D0846196

3 87

César Chávez
UFW Labor Leader

Other titles in the series include:

The 20th Century's
Most Influential
HISPANICS

César Chávez
UFW Labor Leader

by Kevin Hile

LUCENT BOOKS
A part of Gale, Cengage Learning

GALE
CENGAGE Learning·

Detroit • New York • San Francisco • New Haven, Conn • Waterville, Maine • London

GALE
CENGAGE Learning™

LIBRARY OF CONGRESS CATALOGING-IN-PUBLICATION DATA

Hile, Kevin.
  César Chávez : UFW labor leader / by Kevin Hile.
    p. cm. – (The twentieth century's most influential Hispanics)
  Includes bibliographical references and index.
  ISBN 978-1-4205-0094-3 (hardcover)
  1. Chavez, Cesar, 1927-1993. 2. Labor leaders–United States–Biography. 3. Mexican Americans–Biography. 4. Agricultural laborers–Labor unions–United States–History–20th century. 5. United Farm Workers–History. I. Title.
  HD6509.C48H55 2008
  331.88'13092–dc22
  [B]
                                                              2008012505

Lucent Books
27500 Drake Rd
Farmington Hills MI 48331

ISBN-13: 978-1-4205-0094-3
ISBN-10: 1-4205-0094-5

Printed in the United States of America
1 2 3 4 5 6 7 12 11 10 09 08

Table of Contents

Foreword

Hispanics in America and elsewhere have shed humble beginnings to soar to impressive and previously unreachable heights. In the twenty-first century, influential Hispanic figures can be found worldwide and in all fields of endeavor including science, politics, education, the arts, sports, religion, and literature. Some accomplishments, like those of musician Carlos Santana or author Alisa Valdes-Rodriguez, have added a much-needed Hispanic voice to the artistic landscape. Others, such as revolutionary Che Guevara or labor leader Dolores Huerta, have spawned international social movements that have enriched the rights of all peoples.

But who exactly is Hispanic? When studying influential Hispanics, it is important to understand what the term actually means. Unlike strictly racial categories like "black" or "Asian," the term "Hispanic" joins a huge swath of people from different countries, religions, and races. The category was first used by the U.S. census bureau in 1980 and is used to refer to Spanish-speaking people of any race. Officially, it denotes a person whose ancestry either descends in whole or in part from the people of Spain or from the various peoples of Spanish-speaking Latin America. Often the term "Hispanic" is used synonymously with the term "Latino," but the two actually have slightly different meanings. "Latino" refers only to people from the countries of Latin America, such as Argentina, Brazil, and Venezuela, whether they speak Spanish or Portuguese. Meanwhile, Hispanic refers only to Spanish-speaking peoples but from any Spanish-speaking country, such as Spain, Puerto Rico, or Mexico.

In America, Hispanics are reaching new heights of cultural influence, buying power, and political clout. More than 35 million people identified themselves as Hispanic on the 2000 U.S. census, and there were estimated to be more than 41 million Hispanics in America as of 2006. In the twenty-first century people of Hispanic origin have officially become the nation's largest ethnic minority, outnumbering both blacks and Asians. Hispanics constitute about 13 percent of the nation's total population, and by 2050 their numbers are expected to rise to 102.6 million, at which point they would account for 24 percent of the total population. With growing numbers and expanding influence, Hispanic leaders, artists, politicians, and scientists in America and in other countries are commanding attention like never before.

These unique and fascinating stories are the subjects of *The Twentieth Century's Most Influential Hispanics* collection from Lucent Books. Each volume in the series critically examines the challenges, accomplishments, and legacy of influential Hispanic figures; many of whom, like Alberto Gonzales, sprang from modest beginnings to achieve groundbreaking goals. *The Twentieth Century's Most Influential Hispanics* offers vivid narrative, fully documented primary and secondary source quotes, a bibliography, thorough index, and mix of color and black-and-white photographs which enhance each volume and provide excellent starting points for research and discussion.

The Farmworkers' Champion

The right to protest is a key weapon for change in America, as well as in other countries. When political or social forces deny that freedom, there is suffering and injustice. When people who have experienced oppression and prejudice rise up together as one, justice usually prevails. History has shown, however, that the most successful protest efforts were led by strong, charismatic leaders.

One of the most prominent leaders in America in the twentieth century was Martin Luther King Jr., whose voice rallied African Americans and other minorities to fight for their civil rights during the 1950s and 1960s.

At the same time that King was leading his marches and protests, César Chávez was fighting for the rights of Hispanic American farmworkers.

Migrant Hispanic Workers

César Chávez is best known for organizing a workers union called the National Farm Workers of America (NFWA) in 1962. The union is now known as the United Farm Workers (UFW).

Home is a bleak one-room shack for Enos Cervantes and his wife and children, a typical migrant worker family that tended to the farm crops of California in the 1950s.

Based in California, the union was one of the first to successfully fight for the rights of migrant farmworkers, most of whom were of Mexican descent. Migrant workers are people who travel from place to place seeking work. Many migrant workers travel to California, where there is a huge demand for manual labor on the many fruit and vegetable farms.

Large and powerful farming corporations, as well as small family farms, would hire the migrant workers and pay them less than the legal minimum wage. The farm owners were able to pay less because federal and state laws that protected most employees in the United States did not apply to migrant workers. Farm owners were also not legally required to provide a safe working environment, so migrant workers often had to complete their work using improper tools. Portable bathrooms were not provided in the fields, and workers were often exposed to toxic pesticides that made them sick.

As a young man, Chávez worked the fields with his family and later, he worked in them again as an adult. Chávez was a shy and modest person with a big heart. He wanted to help the people in his community to live a better life, so he began to do volunteer work. This led him to do so much more.

Huelga!

Inspired by his parents and by leaders such as Martin Luther King Jr. and India's Mahatma Gandhi, Chávez decided that the farm laborers of California needed better treatment and more rights. He thought they needed a union. In 1962 he created a grassroots campaign to form the National Farm Workers Association (NFWA) by seeking the support and loyalty of the local community.

Chávez was a devout Catholic and a pacifist, so he sought to create change through peaceful means. His favorite tools were the strike and the boycott. Chávez was able to get enough farmworkers to join his union so that they could strike against the big farm companies that oppressed them. They would march and picket companies, chanting "Huelga!" which is Spanish for "Strike!" Chávez also

United Farm Workers members carry signs declaring "Huelga!" (Spanish for "Strike!") while picketing in California's Coachella Valley in 1968.

effectively communicated his mission outside the local community and more people began to support the union by refusing to buy foods such as grapes and lettuce from companies that treated their migrant workers poorly.

Sometimes there was disagreement within Chávez's union. Some people believed that the only way to get the farm companies to change was through violence. Chávez passionately opposed violent strategies, and to prove there were other ways to make a difference, he went on hunger strikes on several occasions. A hunger strike is when someone starves him or herself to protest for a cause. Such strikes can be effective because they draw a lot of media attention. In this way, Chávez sacrificed not only his time and money (he never earned a big salary), but also his body, which some would later speculate led to the union leader's early death at age sixty-six.

Chávez's Legacy

Although Chávez insisted that he was fighting for the rights of *all* migrant workers, regardless of race or religion, most people today see him as a champion of poor Hispanics, especially Mexican Americans. Some people resented Chávez because they believed that he surrounded himself with too many white people as he became an influential labor leader.

Chávez led his cause to many victories, but he also suffered disappointing defeats. As his union merged with the Agricultural Workers Organizing Committee (AWOC) in order to join a federation of unions called the American Federation of Labor and Congress of Industrial Organizations (AFL-CIO), it seemed that Chávez might have compromised some of his ability to lead. He suffered difficult setbacks later in life, such as in 1991 when his union lost a two million dollar lawsuit stemming from a 1979 claim that a strike had financially harmed a company.

Even after the 1960s era of the civil rights movement, Chávez was still able to get a lot accomplished. His tireless devotion to what he always referred to as *La Causa*, or "The Cause," helped to change labor laws for the better.

Chávez was not a writer, and he did not leave behind a lot of books about his beliefs, but many of his speeches were recorded.

César Chávez talks with grape pickers in 1968, promoting the work of the United Farm Workers union. He termed his dedication to improving the lives and working conditions of farm laborers "la causa," or "the cause."

He also told his life story to author Jacques Levy, who wrote *César Chávez: Autobiography of La Causa*. His words from a 1984 speech to the Commonwealth Club of San Francisco aptly summarizes his lifetime hopes:

> All my life, I have been driven by one dream, one goal, one vision: To overthrow a farm labor system in this nation which treats farm workers as if they were not important human beings. Farm workers are not agricultural implements; they are not beasts of burden to be used and discarded. That dream was born in my youth. It was nurtured in my early days of organizing. It has flourished. It has been attacked. . . .
>
> I didn't really appreciate it at the time, but the coming of our union signaled the start of great changes among Hispanics that are only now beginning to be seen.[1]

Chapter 1

A Migrant Childhood

Sometimes people assume that all migrant workers are illegal immigrants from Mexico or other parts of the world. César Chávez, however, was an American citizen, born in the United States just as his father was. The Chávezes were all hard-working people with strong beliefs in community involvement and in their Catholic faith. Both Chávez's mother and father served as strong role models. Their lessons stayed with Chávez for the rest of his life.

During the first decades of the twentieth century, the Chávez family was fairly prosperous. Chávez's grandfather, Césario, came to the United States from the Mexican state of Chihuahua. He left his country to avoid being drafted into the army. At the time, the government often forced people to join the army, and in Césario's home state this meant that he had a good chance of being killed by Apache Indians.

Césario moved to Arizona and worked a variety of jobs before establishing his own farm not far from the city of Yuma. He had fourteen children, including César Chávez's father, Librado, who was known as Lenny. Of all his siblings, Lenny was the only one who stayed on his parent's farm to live and work. He married Juana

César Chávez

Estrada, who had immigrated to the United States with her family when she was just an infant of six months. Together, they inherited the farm from Lenny's family and ventured into other businesses, including a grocery store, a pool hall, and an auto repair shop. Their home was in the same building as the store.

César Chávez was born in his family's home on March 31, 1927. Named after his grandfather and his mother's family, his full given name was Césario Estrada Chávez. He was the second child born to the Chávezes, who eventually had five children, including Rita, Richard, Vicky, and Lenny.

Happy Early Days

The Chávezes struggled somewhat to provide for their children, but César would later recall these early years as some of the happiest of his life. Their home lacked indoor plumbing and electricity, but there was always food and shelter. He once described these days in an interview with author Studs Terkel as "a strange life. We had been poor, but we knew every night there was a bed *there*, and that *this* was our room. There was a kitchen. It was sort of a settled life, and we had chickens and hogs, eggs and all those things."[2]

Greatly in need of money during the Depression, the Chávez family moved to California because of the available work as farm laborers. Pictured is a migrant family in similar circumstances as the Chávez family.

Chávez enjoyed the farm life, especially playing with his brother Richard and his cousin Manuel, who were about his age. They climbed the trees on the farm and played games in the fields.

These were the early years of the Great Depression, which began in America in 1929 after the stock market crashed and the economy slumped. The Chávez family managed to do fairly well, however, because they grew food on their farm that they could eat.

Césario Becomes César at School

"The teachers were Anglos and school was in English, but I would say 95 percent of the people in the village of Gila were our relatives, and there were only a few families that were not Spanish-speaking. But the teacher thought nothing of changing our names the moment we were in class. She wouldn't pronounce his real name—which is Césario—she cut it to César right away."

Rita Chávez Medina, quoted in Jacques Levy, *César Chávez: Autobiography of La Causa*. New York: Norton, 1975, p. 21.

There was also money from their businesses. The kindness of Chávez's mother and father, however, led to their undoing, in a way. Because many of their customers were friends and relatives who had been hit hard by the Depression, they were willing to offer them goods and services on credit. Out of the goodness of their hearts, they told people they could pay them later when they had the money.

This resulted in the Chávezes being owed a great deal of money that they were unlikely to see any time soon. Meanwhile, they had their own bills to pay. The financial situation only got worse when they lost their harvest due to drought and they had no vegetables to sell. The drought was so bad, that much of the farmland in the central plains and part of the west became known as the dust bowl. The Chávezes were far from the only people to suffer from the lack of rain.

Forced Off Their Land

Lenny Chávez asked the local bank for a loan so he would not lose his farm, but the bank refused. In desperate need of money, the Chávez patriarch made a fateful decision to travel to California in 1937, where he heard farms were hiring migrant workers. At first, he went by himself, leaving his wife and children in Arizona. The rest of his family later joined him, however.

Once in California, the entire family worked to make money. They lived in Oxnard, near Los Angeles, for a while, picking beans and peas while Chávez's mother made money knitting clothes she would then sell.

The money they raised was barely enough to keep them alive, let alone keep their Arizona farm safe from repossession. So in 1937 Lenny traveled to Phoenix, Arizona, where he tried to convince the state government to loan him enough money to survive the hard times.

An information booth at a farm labor camp in California provides assistance to a family of migrant workers, who flooded the state during the Dust Bowl.

Lenny Chávez was refused again, however, and this time it cost the family everything. The farm was taken away from them and auctioned off on February 6, 1939. Chávez remembers this as one of the saddest days in his life, especially when he saw the farm's new owner tearing up the trees on which he and his brother and cousin once climbed. He would remember this day as a time when big business and government defeated the hopes of a poor, honest, and hard-working man.

Life of the Migrant

After they lost the farm, the Chávez's returned to California and the migrant life. Even so, Lenny never gave up hope of one day returning to Arizona and buying a new farm. Chávez often

The Tractor Comes

After their home was auctioned off in February 1939, the new owner had parts of the Chávez homestead bulldozed. Chávez recalls the humiliating experience:

I remember the tractor heading for the corral. I shudder now to think of it. It was there that Richard and I had fun together riding the horses and the young calves bareback. Or at least we did until one calf bucked and threw Richard right through the pole fence. It was in that corral, too, that I first got on the big dapple gray stallion that nobody would ride because he was too spirited. One day I put a rope hitch around his muzzle and jumped on his back. He only bucked a little, and from then on I could ride him. . . .

Now the tractor was at the corral, and the old sturdy fence posts gave way as easily as stalks of corn. It was a monstrous thing. . . . [Richard and I] didn't blame the grower, we blamed the poor tractor driver. We just thought he was mean. I wanted to go stop him but I couldn't. I felt helpless.

Quoted in Jacques Levy, *César Chávez: Autobiography of La Causa*. New York: Norton, 1975, pp. 41–42.

heard his parents talking about this dream in an effort to get their hopes up. He said:

> [My father] had been used to owning the land and all of a sudden there was no more land. What I heard . . . what I made out of conversations between my mother and my father—things like, we'll work this season and then we'll get enough money and we'll go and buy a piece of land in Arizona. Things like that. Became like a habit. He never gave up hope that someday he would come back and get a little piece of land. . . . These conversations were sort of melancholy. I guess my brothers and my sisters could also see this very sad look on my father's face.[3]

For the next several years, the Chávezes moved from town to town in California, always hoping to find farm work. First they went to Atascadero, then to Gonzales, and then to Half Moon Bay. Lenny Chávez worked at vineyards, cherry orchards, and bean

Harsh living conditions met migrant workers who moved west to tend farms in California during the Dust Bowl. This family uses tents for shelter after moving to the San Joaquin Valley in 1937.

farms, and his family helped, too, working the fields. Many other towns followed: Brawley, Mendota, Wasco, King City, Delano, Salinas, Kingsburg, McFarland, and Selma. At one time, while the family was living in Oxnard, they had to endure living in a tent during the winter. Through his family's misfortune, Chávez became intimately knowledgeable of what it meant to be a migrant worker.

Early Education

During all these moves, young Chávez continued to attend school, which he had not started until he was seven years old. His parents, who were illiterate, believed in education and that it would help their children live better lives. But school was hard for Chávez because the lessons were all in English. At home, he only spoke Spanish, and while he tried very hard to learn English in class, sometimes his teachers would punish or criticize him if he lapsed back into Spanish or made a mistake in English.

Worse than being criticized by his teachers was the feeling that they all thought he was somehow stupid. Chávez knew his fellow Mexican Americans suffered the same humiliations. "We were like monkeys in a cage. There were lots of racist remarks that still hurt my ears when I think of them. And we couldn't do anything except sit there and take it."[4] Because of such treatment, Chávez came to hate school. It was also hard for him to adjust to school, because his family moved so often. By the time he was in the eighth grade, he had attended thirty-seven schools.

During this time, however, Chávez was receiving another kind of education that was perhaps much more valuable. He loved to listen to his grandparents and uncles read to him from books in Spanish, and he especially loved learning from his mother. In *The Words of César Chávez* Richard J. Jensen and John C. Hammerback, explain:

> Chávez's mother kept the family unified. She taught her children through traditional knowledge contained in *dichos* (proverbs and sayings), *consejos* (advice), and *cuentos* (stories) that often carried a moral les-

son. They covered a wide range of subjects, some telling of miracles, others promoting obedience and honesty. The sayings and stories, an integral part of the Mexican American culture, would later appear in his speeches and writings. He used them to teach all audiences and especially to instruct and identify with his Mexican American audiences.[5]

César Quits School

"[In 1942] César graduated from school, and he told my mother, 'From now on, Mother, you're not going to step one foot out of the house to work anymore!' So my mom said, 'No, I want you to go to high school.' He said, 'No, I'd rather not go to school. I'd rather see you home.' She was pretty old, too. So she just stayed home and did the cleaning and the washing and the cooking, and we used to work."

Rita Chávez Medina, quoted in Jacques Levy, *César Chávez: Autobiography of La Causa.* New York: Norton, 1975, p. 72.

Sal Si Puedes

Finally, the Chávezes ended up in a place called Sal Si Puedes in San Jose, California. *Sal Si Puedes* is Spanish for "Get Out If You Can," and by the look of the place, Chávez could see how it got its name. "The nickname came about because it seemed as though the only way young men left Sal Si Puedes was to go off to jail, the military, or the cemetery,"[6] he later told people.

The place was a barrio, another name for a neighborhood where mostly Spanish-speaking people lived. Most of the homes were poorly constructed shacks. There were no proper sewers and no electricity. Although back on his family's farm, Chávez had no problem living without these conveniences, in Sal Si Puedes it added to the feeling of hopelessness.

In addition to the poor pay the Hispanic workers were making, life was made more difficult by the prejudice they faced from whites, or "Anglos," as the Hispanics called them. It was common at the time to see signs in the windows of stores and restaurants declaring that "No Negroes or Mexicans" were allowed inside. Some signs combined this warning with one saying that no dogs were allowed, either, implying that Mexicans and blacks were on the same level as dogs.

Such prejudice could be found not only in San Jose, but also in towns all across California. In India, California, railroad tracks separated the white part of town from the Hispanic part. One day Chávez and his brothers tried to cross the tracks to go to a hamburger place, but the police quickly arrived and sent them back to what they called Mexican town.

Chávez's Parents

Chávez's father did not believe in tolerating such indignities. He was willing to fight for himself and others like him, and

Striking with His Father

Chávez's first exposure to striking and unions came when he was old enough to start working the fields with his father. These early strikes were usually unsuccessful, but Chávez learned from them. Successful strikes against the growers could only come if the workers were brave enough and resolved enough to stick together until the company gave in to their demands. Chávez recalls his first strike:

Our first direct experience with a union strike was in 1948, I think. . . . As I recall, we struck for a few days, and then people began to leave the strike. Pretty soon there were just a handful of us, and the strike was over.

But those first few days we were really faced with a lot of people, big rallies. I think all of us were geared to getting large crowds out there. Somehow it was planted in our minds that if we didn't get a lot of people, we weren't going to win. So the moment the numbers dropped, people got frightened and began to leave. It's a very difficult thing to overcome. People are very poor, and they can't stay off work for long.

Quoted in Jacques Levy, *César Chávez: Autobiography of La Causa*. New York: Norton, 1975, p. 79.

he proved this in 1937 by joining a union called the United Cannery, Agricultural, Packing and Allied Workers of America (UCAPAW). The union members quickly organized a strike, but they found they lacked the resources to survive without working. The strike was called off, and the union dissolved.

Lenny Chávez did not give up, however. He continued to join unions time and time again. Chávez recalled how his father and siblings lost many jobs because Lenny would walk away from work in order to protest that someone else was being treated unfairly:

> We were among the families who always honored somebody else's grievance. Somebody would have a personal grievance with the employer: He'd say I'm not gonna work for this man. Even though we were working, we'd honor it. We felt we had to. So we'd walk out, too. Because we were prepared to honor those things . . . . If we were picking at a piece rate [growers would often pay laborers based on the weight of the crops they picked] and we knew they were cheating on the weight, we wouldn't stand for it. So we'd lose the job, and we'd go elsewhere. There were other families like that.[7]

Chávez's father was not the only one who sacrificed himself and his family for the sake of others. His mother would gladly give whatever she could to people in need. As a staunch Catholic, she believed in charity wholeheartedly. Another aspect of her faith was her belief in nonviolence.

"She would always talk to us about not fighting, not responding in kind," [8] Chávez recalled. This was a very different attitude from the culture of machismo common in many Hispanic communities. Chávez knew many boys and men who believed fighting back was the sign of a true man, but his mother instilled in him her own, more peaceful methods of solving conflicts.

Years later, Chávez would draw on his religious beliefs as a source of strength, not only for himself, but also for the entire Mexican American community. He also viewed the Catholic Church itself as a powerful ally in the fight for justice for the poor. As he said in a speech in 1968:

The Church . . . is a tremendously powerful institution in our society, and in the world. That Church is one form of the Presence of God on Earth, and so naturally it is powerful. It is powerful by definition. It is a powerful moral and spiritual force which cannot be ignored by any movement.[9]

A Brief Rebellious Period

As a teenager, Chávez was not a completely obedient young man. He had a willful streak and he asserted his own unique tastes in music and clothing. Instead of listening to traditional Mexican music, he liked the big band music that was popular in the 1940s. He also liked the outfits called zoot suits that the

Two injured young men draw a crowd after being assaulted by servicemen in 1943 Los Angeles. Such incidents were labeled "Zoot Suit Riots" after the style of clothing favored by the Hispanic youths who were victims of such attacks.

Latino pachucos (young, cool Hispanic men) wore. Filipinos and some African Americans also wore zoot suits, which were characterized by baggy pants and long coats made from silk.

Young men who wore zoot suits were considered gang members and criminals by police and white society in general. Chávez and his friends were repeatedly harassed just for wearing the clothing, which they considered stylish. In 1943 there was even a zoot-suit riot in Los Angeles, where whites attacked and beat up Mexican youths simply because of the way they were dressed.

After graduating from the eighth grade in 1942, Chávez decided to leave school, much to the dismay of his mother . His main excuse was that he wanted to support his family since his father had been in a car accident and could not work, but he was probably glad to get out of the classroom where he had experienced so much prejudice.

Meeting Helen and Joining the Navy

From 1942 until 1944, Chávez worked long hours in the fields. During this time, he and his family were living in Delano, California. Here he met Helen Fabela. Helen worked at a grocery store, and the two became friends and started to date. When they could afford to, they went to the movie theater in town.

Chávez was growing restless, however. His life as a farmworker was boring him. In 1944, he turned seventeen and he decided he wanted to serve in the military, hoping the experience would add some excitement in his life. Excitement would be easy to find since the United States was deeply involved in World War II.

Chávez enlisted in the U.S. Navy and his parents were very upset because they did not want their son to go to war. He decided on the navy because he thought naval service would be less dangerous than being in the army. He also reasoned that he would have been drafted anyway.

The navy and the young Mexican American were not a good fit. There was a definite racial divide in which white men were given the chance to fight for America, while Mexican Americans were assigned duties such as cleaning, maintaining grounds and equipment, and painting the ships. For the two years he was in the U.S.

Navy, Chávez never participated in any military action. Instead, he was assigned to a ship that performed weather patrols near Saipan and also served as a destroyer escort.

One positive side effect of being in the navy was that Chávez became interested in photography. He won a used camera in a poker game with his shipmates, and from that time on became a shutterbug. Many of the photos later taken of his union's activities were taken by Chávez himself.

A Taste of Peaceful Resistance

While still in the service, Chávez was occasionally granted leave. He would return to Delano to visit family and friends, including Helen. One night in 1944, he and Helen decided to go to the movies. It would be an unpleasant experience, although an educational one for Chávez.

Like many businesses in California at the time, the theater was segregated, with one section for whites and one for Mexicans and other minorities. The only place to sit that night was in the whites-only section. An usher told Chávez he had to move, but his stubborn streak kicked in over this injustice and he refused. The theater called the police, who tried to throw César and Helen out. Still, Chávez refused. A police officer tried to intimidate him, but although the theater had a segregation policy, there was no law that said Chávez had to move. In the end Chávez and Helen were allowed to stay, and Chávez had won a clear moral victory.

After World War II ended in 1945, Chávez remained in the navy. He decided to leave in 1946 and was honorably discharged. Having gained nothing from his military experience, there was really only one option left to him: to return to farm work. This may have seemed a dismal prospect for the young man, but as he returned to the fields of Delano, he brought with him the idealistic beliefs that would seed a new hope for migrant workers everywhere.

Chapter 2

Becoming a Leader

When he returned to California in 1946 after serving in the navy, César Chávez had no grand plans for becoming a labor union organizer. Having known only hardship, hunger, and long hours of work, he assumed he was returning to his old life. Chávez was an unassuming and modest young man, soft-spoken and rather shy. In short, he was not very charismatic and not someone who would clearly stand out as a community leader, let alone a person who would one day gain national attention and get his face on the cover of *Time* magazine.

He did, however, have a stubborn streak in him, and an innate sense that the abuse farmworkers suffered had to change. He just did not know what to do to enact that change and later he would say:

> We thought the only way we could get out of the circle of poverty was to work our way up and send our kids to college. That's the trap most poor people get themselves into. It's easier for a person to just escape, to get out of poverty, than to change the situation.[10]

Back in the Fields

Back in Delano, Chávez worked in cotton fields and vineyards, and he resumed dating Helen. The two married on October 22, 1948. For their honeymoon, Chávez borrowed the family car and took his new bride on a tour of California missions.

Returning to Delano, he got a job picking grapes in the summer, and in the winter he worked the cotton fields. He and Helen moved into a tiny building. Chávez recalled:

> We had a one-room shack without electricity or running water. It was bitterly cold, and we only had one of those little kerosene camping stoves, which we kept turned on day and night with water on it. But that stove didn't heat anything. We were miserable. When we stepped out of the shack, we stepped right into mud—thick, black clay. Since I was without a car, I had to ask for rides to jobs that were four, five, six, ten miles away from the camp.[11]

Migrant farm workers and their families typically lived in miserable conditions in shacks like these or in other substandard housing, including tents or converted busses.

After a while, Chávez and Helen left Delano for San Jose, where Chávez's younger brother Richard was able to give him a job on an apricot orchard. Other jobs followed, including a two-year period as a strawberry field sharecropper outside San Jose, but there was no money to be made when the harvest turned sour.

Ross Meets Chávez

"At the very first meeting, I was very much impressed with César. I could tell he was intensely interested, a kind of burning interest rather than one of those inflammatory things that lasts one night and is then forgotten. He asked many questions, part of it to see if I really knew, putting me to the test. But it was much more than that. . . . He made the connections very quickly between the civic weakness of the group and the social neglect in the barrio, and also conversely, what could be done about the social neglect once the power was developed."

Quoted in Jacques Levy, *César Chávez: Autobiography of La Causa*. New York: Norton, 1975, p. 102.

Chávez next moved to Crescent City in northern California, where he and his brother Richard and three cousins worked at a lumber mill. The rainy, chilly weather got to him, though, and he returned to Sal Si Puedes and the sunnier weather. Putting his experience to good use, Chávez got another job at a lumber mill. By this time, Chávez had three children to support: Fernando, Sylvia, and Linda.

Father McDonnell

In 1952 there was still no church in Sal Si Puedes, and this was the reason Father Donald McDonnell came to the settlement. He convinced the San Francisco Archdiocese to let him work and live in Sal Si Puedes and attend to the large population of Catholic Mexican workers.

Since Chávez was a devout Catholic, he soon met Father McDonnell and the two men became close friends. They shared

Indian leader Mahatma Gandhi promoted peaceful resistance while seeking to end British rule of his country. He was an important role model for César Chávez, who insisted on accomplishing his goal of improving the lives of farm workers through nonviolent means.

not only a religious devotion, but they were also about the same age and cared about the poor. Chávez began spending a lot of time with the priest and helping him out. Knowing carpentry, he did maintenance work at the church, but he also accompanied the father when he visited jails and *bracero* camps to perform mass. Bracero is another name for migrant workers from Mexico, especially agricultural workers.

One of the first tasks Chávez and McDonnell undertook was helping some of the local people claim deceased relatives from the nearby hospital so that they could be buried near their homes. Surprisingly, there was a great deal of red tape to go through at the hospital just to do this, but Father McDonnell knew the law and was able to help families claim the bodies.

It was Father McDonnell who encouraged Chávez to read, too.

While Chávez had learned to read in school, he was rather slow at it. Still, the books Father McDonnell gave him inspired him, and he paged through them steadily. Chávez read about important religious figures such as Saint Francis of Assisi, as well as more contemporary figures. He was greatly influenced by the story of Mahatma Gandhi, the famous pacifist who led India out of British rule. Gandhi served as a model for Chávez for the rest of his life.

Fred Ross and the CSO

In addition to his church work, Father McDowell was a leader in the Community Service Organization (CSO), a group founded by Saul Alinsky. The organizer of the CSO was Fred Ross. Ross had studied teaching in college, but after graduating had turned to social work when he could not find a teaching job. Before World War II, he worked with the Okies (white migrant workers who came to California from Oklahoma to work the farms during the Great Depression), and so helping Hispanic migrant workers was not a great stretch for him.

Chávez's Bombshell

"We were all so sad. Fred and I were crying, and I guess the only one that was not was César. As the convention ended, he got up and said, 'I have an announcement to make. I resign.' He dropped the bombshell on the convention. He had so much guts! Everybody was pressuring him to stay. People were crying. But he didn't bow to the pressure. He left. Later when César told me, 'I'm going to start my own Union,' I was just appalled, the thought was so overwhelming. But when the initial shock wore off, I thought it was exciting."

Dolores Huerta, on learning of Chávez's decision to leave the CSO when it voted against organizing a farmworkers' union. Quoted in Jacques Levy, *César Chávez: Autobiography of La Causa*. New York: Norton, 1975, p. 147.

The purpose of the CSO was to get Hispanic workers to become politically active, primarily by voting. Ross felt that Chávez could do a lot to help organize the local community, who already knew Chávez well.

At first, Chávez was reluctant. Ross was a white man from Los Angeles, and Chávez did not believe that the CSO leader really understood what the migrant workers were going through. His wife, Helen, felt that her husband and Ross should meet, and when they did, Chávez was surprised by how well Ross listened and seemed sincerely sympathetic to their needs.

Chávez agreed to work in the CSO. Employment at the mill was haphazard at best, and he devoted his time not spent in the fields to helping Ross and McDowell grow the CSO's membership. The U.S. presidential election between Democratic candidate Adlai Stevenson and Republican Dwight D. Eisenhower was coming up, and the CSO was supporting many local candidates who were running for office. Chávez traveled from home to home, getting people to register to vote or, if they were not yet U.S. citizens, convincing them to apply for citizenship.

When the lumber mill cut workers and let Chávez go, he decided to work full time for the CSO. At thirty-five dollars a week, it was not a great-paying job, but it was a job he believed in much more than harvesting cotton or cutting lumber.

The Organizer

Every night for the two months before the national election, Chávez pounded the pavement and talked to potential voters. Ross was so impressed, that he put Chávez in charge of the voter registration drive. He signed up more than four thousand new voters.

Ross's confidence in his new right-hand man was growing. He gave Chávez more and more responsibilities. He told the young organizer to go to Oakland, near San Francisco, and hold house meetings to tell people about the CSO and voting.

Overwhelmed by the city, which was much larger than San Jose, Chávez was sometimes late to meetings when he got directions wrong and lost his way. When he did find the meeting, he was invited in without much fanfare and would sit quietly among the guests. His first meeting, which was in West Oakland, was an inauspicious beginning. For a long time, he sat among a bunch of women homemakers, who were wondering when the CSO representative would show up.

Chávez recalled what happened when he finally screwed up his courage and announced that he was the organizer, and one of the women reacted negatively:

> She looked at me and said, "Umph!" I could tell what she meant, a snotty kid, a kid organizer, you're kidding! That meeting was a disaster, really a disaster. I fumbled all over the place. . . . But toward the end of the meeting they were listening to me, and I got them to promise to hold house meetings . . . and to commit

Union organizers promoted their cause in small home meetings and in larger group settings, such as this gathering of migrant farm workers in the late 1950s.

themselves. Probably they felt sorry for me more than anything else.[12]

Drawing Attention

In the 1950s there was a lot of fear about communism. Communism is a form of government in which a single political party controls all aspects of society. Communist governments control all goods and methods of production in countries they rule. In theory, the government distributes resources equally among all the citizens of the country. Communist governments and democratic governments usually oppose each other. U.S. senator Eugene McCarthy, who headed the U.S. House Un-American Activities Committee at the time, had spread fear among Americans that communist spies were everywhere. Because Chávez was a liberal supporting the poor and fair-employment rights, many business owners, and especially Republican politicians, suspected he was a communist.

Republicans, who knew that most Hispanics would be voting for Democrats, began to harass people waiting in line to vote. Ross had enough and contacted the U.S. attorney general, J. Howard McGrath, to protest. Chávez was brave enough to sign the message that was sent to McGrath when most of his colleagues, fearing reprisals, would not.

The result was a standoff between Republicans in California and the CSO that was reported in newspapers. The Republicans accused the CSO of illegal voter registration practices, such as putting the names of noncitizens and dead people on ballots, and the CSO accused Republicans of being racists.

All the publicity got Chávez attention, and soon even the FBI was interested. They contacted him one day at work, and took Chávez to a meeting with the Republican Central Committee. The meeting quickly fell apart, with both sides screaming at each other. "That was the first time I started shouting at Anglos, shouting back at them,"[13] he recalled.

Neighbors who knew what Chávez was doing started calling him "the politician." Although he knew it to be a half-insult, because politicians were far from trusted, Chávez took the name-

Communist Accusations

During the 1952 presidential election, Republicans in California were concerned about the CSO's role in getting more Hispanic farmworkers to vote because they tended to vote the Democratic ticket. The FBI harassed Chávez regularly, asking him what organizations he belonged to. This soon became common knowledge among the field-workers, who grew afraid of talking to Chávez because it might make others suspect they were communists, too. Chávez recalled that "the Chicanos wouldn't talk to me. They were afraid. . . . Everywhere I went to organize they would bluntly ask, 'Are you a Communist?'"

In frustration, Chávez talked to Father McDonnell, who, together with other area Catholic priests, formally announced that Chávez was not a communist and that he had their blessing. According to Susan Ferris and Ricardo Sandoval, "The Church's endorsement helped Chávez grow into an authority figure in his new job as a full-time organizer."

Quoted from Susan Ferris and Ricardo Sandoval, eds., *The Fight in the Fields: César Chávez and the Farmworkers Movement.* New York: Harcourt, Brace., 1997, p. 49.

calling lightly. The label was partly a way of teasing him, too, for being a young upstart.

More Communist Fears and Prejudice

Perhaps more of a wake-up call for Chávez was the fact that many people, even several priests, suspected him of being a communist, too. While on a trip to Madera in 1953, Chávez was confronted by a priest who accused him of being a communist, and after that it was nearly impossible for the young CSO campaigner to talk to potential new members.

Another surprise for Chávez was that some of the people in the Hispanic community he wanted to meet refused to talk with him if he brought along African American members. Although most of the migrant farmworkers were Hispanic, Chávez never saw the

CSO as an organization for Mexican Americans alone. He wanted to fight for all the migrant farmworkers, who had no say in how they were treated.

There was also a schism between Catholics and Protestants within the organization. People not only saw the CSO as primarily Hispanic, but also as primarily Catholic. And so when Chávez and Ross recruited Protestants freely into their group, as well as Jews, some people objected. Chávez stressed that the CSO was not a religious organization affiliated with any church; it was a political activism group. It was hard to overcome these racial and religious prejudices, as well as the fear people had of being labeled a communist if they joined the CSO.

Chávez was steadfast. He organized citizenship classes, house meetings, and registration drives. Through stubborn determination, he was making headway.

The First Union Involvement

Although the work he was doing was helping laborers a great deal, Chávez was not really thinking about organizing a union, even by the mid-1950s. In 1958, however, Ross suggested that the CSO do something to help the Packinghouse Workers Union in Oxnard, where the union hoped to organize workers in the lemon industry.

Chávez was uneasy about this involvement. Recalling his younger days with his family in Oxnard, he knew these people needed help, but he was not confident the CSO was the right group to assist them. The union was having trouble keeping its membership up because of failures at the negotiating table, and union president Ralph Hellstein thought the CSO's ability to recruit was just what they needed.

Despite his vocal doubts, Chávez agreed to assist them. He spent 1958 and 1959 organizing house meetings and voter registration.

Eventually Chávez learned that the real issue preventing the union from organizing farm laborers and getting them employed was the braceros, or Mexican migrant workers. The U.S. government started a program during World War II called the Bracero Program. It allowed Mexican workers into the United States legally to fill in for U.S. agricultural workers who were fighting in the war.

The war ended in 1948, but the Bracero Program continued, mostly because it benefited the growers. The Mexican workers would work for less money and for longer hours. Meeting after meeting, Chávez would hear people complain about the braceros, but he dodged the issue, not sure how to deal with it. Eventually he did:

> Finally I decided this was the issue I had to tackle. The fact that braceros also were farm workers didn't bother me. There's an old dicho, no puede dejar Dios

A Workaholic

Chávez was a workaholic, often getting by on little food and sleep as he worked for the CSO and, later, for his own union. His commitment came at great personal expense, however. Chávez admitted that he could neglect his wife and children when he worked long hours. During the fight with the Farm Placement Service, he had lost twenty-five pounds. Chávez said:

> Not only that, but I nearly lost my youngest son, Birdy, who was born that August. He got diarrhea when he was about two weeks old, and I was too busy to take him to the doctor. Finally Helen walked with him to an osteopath, who misread the symptoms. She took him home and called me. She was crying. Then I realized how worried she was, and we rushed him to the hospital where the doctors said he wasn't going to live. In desperation I said, "Doctor, how

about getting someone to consult with you." The doctor got a pediatrician from Ventura who diagnosed the problem and was able to stop the diarrhea. Birdy was saved.

Quoted in Jacques Levy, *César Chávez: Autobiography of La Causa.* New York: Norton, 1975, p. 143.

César Chávez, right, stands next to his wife, Helen, and six of their eight children. Chávez's work with la causa *often meant spending significant time away from his family.*

por Dios—you can't exchange one god for another. This was a question of justice, and I've never had any problem making a decision like that.[14]

Fighting the Farm Placement Service

In tackling the issue of braceros, Chávez knew that the law was on his side, but that the farms and local politicians were not. Farm owners were supposed to hire local people first, and only resort to hiring braceros if no one else could be found. But farm employers had a trick up their sleeve. Laborers who requested work in Oxnard in the morning were told they had to go to the Farm Placement Service office 8 miles (13km) away and register to work for the day. By the time the worker did so and returned, the braceros had taken all the jobs for the day. The registration

Mexicans employed by the Bracero Program, an agreement between the U.S. and Mexico to supply California farms with workers, tend to a chili pepper crop in California in 1964.

form was only good for the one day, so if the job seeker came back the next day, he would be sent to the Farm Placement Service Office again. This was how employers avoided hiring more expensive local workers in favor of the braceros, who were more easily exploited.

Researching the law and trying to apply for work himself at the bracero camp, Chávez figured out what was going on firsthand. He began making careful records of his experiences, documenting what was going on. He recruited others to come with him to the Farm Placement Service office, and together they would spend hours filling out unnecessarily complicated and detailed forms. They knew the forms were useless in getting them jobs, but now Chávez had even more records from other people, not just himself.

Chávez organized meetings with the director of the Southern California branch of the Farm Placement Service and with a representative of the Bureau of Employment Security; he contacted the state governor's office to file grievances, but nothing was done. Finally, he decided there had to be an organized protest.

The First March

By staging a sit-in protest in April 1959 at one of the area's largest farms that hired braceros, Chávez created a sensation. The farmer reacted to the hundreds of protestors just as Chávez had hoped: he police were called and a federal official was on the scene. Seeing what was happening, the official ordered the farmer to send the braceros home and hire the local workers. This was done as ordered, but within hours after the police and officials left the new employees were fired for alleged incompetence.

Undaunted, Chávez staged a march the very next day. This time, not only were the police present, but also the media. In front of the cameras, Chávez gave a speech and he and his followers burned the Farm Placement Service referral cards to demonstrate their point.

The next month Chávez's group picketed in Ventura during a visit from U.S. secretary of labor James Mitchell, followed by a march through the town. The police threatened to put them in jail. Chávez dared them to, and they backed off.

His next strategy was to overwhelm the Farm Placement Service with over a hundred documented, formal complaints of local laborers who were refused work. Chávez received encouragement from John Carr, the director of California's Department of Employment, to keep pressing Edward Hayes, the director of the Farm Placement Service, for answers. None came, but Chávez could tell Hayes was feeling pressure.

Soon, Chávez had laborers from all across the region contacting him, and he told them to go to the farms, find braceros who were taking their jobs, and then send in their complaints to the Farm Placement Service. The strategy worked, and employers were beginning to bend to Chávez's pressure to hire locals and pay them ninety cents per hour, which was up from the usual sixty-five to seventy-five cents.

The cherry on top of this progress came when the director of the Southern California Farm Placement Service, William Cunningham, was investigated and accused of taking bribes from the farm industry. He was fired and lost his pension.

Last Years at the CSO

The CSO promoted Chávez to general director in 1958, and the next year they named him executive director. He moved his family to East Los Angeles to take up his new responsibilities. Chávez spent the next three years there, continuing his work and growing the CSO membership. The organization was gaining national attention, not only because of Chávez, but also because of the work of people like Dolores "Lola" Huerta, who headed the Sacramento office and became the CSO's vice president and lobbyist.

The mission of the CSO had always been to improve the lives of minority workers, especially Hispanics, in California. Most people in the CSO felt that the emphasis should be to help those living in the cities. Chávez, whose roots were in the country, had his heart set on focusing his efforts on farm laborers. "César had always talked about organizing farm workers," recalled his wife, Helen, "even before the CSO. After all, we were both farm workers, and my parents and his parents and our whole families."[15]

Chávez had even turned down a much higher-paying job with the Agricultural Workers Organizing Committee (AWOC) because he knew that organization was so large that he would not be allowed the freedom he needed to achieve his own goals. Also, the members of the AWOC were mostly white, and Chávez knew this would be a disadvantage in recruiting the mostly Mexican American farmworkers. Instead, he repeatedly tried to convince the CSO to support the creation of a farmworkers' union, but his motion was repeatedly voted down.

Finally, after the CSO's convention in 1962, Chávez made a last-ditch effort to pass his union idea. Once again denied, he felt it was time to make a decision. He announced that he was resigning.

Chávez did not make this decision lightly. He had been dedicated to the CSO for ten years, but he felt he had no other choice. With its increasing success, the CSO was also forgetting its grass-roots heritage and becoming mainstream. Chávez reflected:

> Doctors, lawyers and politicians began joining. They would get elected to some office in the organization and then, for all practical purposes, leave. Intent on using the CSO for their own prestige purposes, these "leaders," may of them, lacked the urgency we had to have. . . . So I started a revolt within the CSO. I refused to sit at the head table at meetings, refused to wear a suite and tie, and finally I even refused to shave and cut my hair. It used to embarrass some of the professionals. At every meeting I got up and gave my standard speech: we shouldn't meet in fancy motels, we were getting away from the people, farmworkers had to be organized. But nothing happened. In March of '62 I resigned and came to Delano to begin organizing the [San Joaquin] Valley on my own.[16]

Chapter 3

La Causa

Anyone with less devotion than Chávez might have accused him of being both rash and irresponsible. In 1962 he had a wife and eight children to support, and quitting the CSO meant he had no job and only twelve hundred dollars in savings to fall back on. It was as if he was beginning all over again from scratch.

But, he was back doing what he loved: organizing farmworkers at a grassroots level. He started by getting the support of his family and friends, including his brother Richard, cousin Manuel, and Dolores Huerta. Huerta worked for the CSO, but she offered to help Chávez on the weekends. Manuel and Richard had both found jobs outside the farm industry: Manuel in car sales and Richard in construction. At first, they balked at Chávez's request to join him because they believed they had escaped the endless poverty of farm work for better lives. Chávez, however, convinced them by reminding them of their roots and that they could be part of the solution. Otherwise, farmworkers might never gain a better life. He also gained the loyalty of Reverend James Drake, a Protestant minister who had come to Delano as part of the interdenominational California Migrant Ministry.

Founding the National Farm Workers Association

Now back in the familiar town of Delano, Chávez got down to work while his wife earned money picking grapes and taking odd jobs. While most of his children were in school, Chávez would drive around the valley, organizing house meetings and building interested in his idea for a new union, which he called *La Causa* (The Cause). He took his youngest son, Anthony (nicknamed Birdy), with him because he was too little to go to school. "It's very difficult to ask your wife and children to make a sacrifice," he recalled. "And it's unfair to some extent. You must want to do something very badly. But I had no difficulty in that decision, Helen wanted to do it. In that respect I was free. And the kids were a lot smaller. . . . They were brought up with the Cause and had to suffer with us."[17]

When he felt that they had aroused enough interest through the house meetings and other recruitment efforts, Chávez sent out requests for people to select representatives to send to an organiza-

Delegates representing several farming regions gather at the founding meeting of the National Farm Workers Association on September 30, 1962 in Fresno, California.

tional meeting. Before the meeting, he felt that it was important to create an easy-to-recognize symbol under which to rally. He chose an eagle similar to the one on the Mexican flag. According to Peter Matthiessen:

> Some people like to think that the eagle appeared to César Chávez in a dream; some say it came to Chávez's cousin Manuel, whose inspiration was the label on a wine jug of Gallo Thunderbird. The truth is that the emblem Chávez wanted was an Aztec eagle, which he asked Manuel to design.[18]

Because the black eagle was surrounded by red, some people said it looked like a Nazi or communist logo, but the color scheme was chosen because red and black flags are carried in Mexico by strikers.

The founding meeting of the National Farm Workers Association (NFWA) was held on September 30, 1962, at a movie theater in Fresno, California. It was attended by 287 people. Here, Chávez clearly stated his goals for the union members: a wage increase to $1.50 per hour, life and unemployment insurance, and the creation of a credit union from which members could get loans. The insurance and credit union would be funded by monthly dues, boosted by Richard Chávez's generosity in mortgaging his own house so they would have funds to loan.

The Grassroots Method

Chávez did not want the NFWA to operate like the CSO or AWOC, with decisions coming down from a remote headquarters office. He wanted the membership to have as much say as possible and to participate actively; he also wanted the union to be self-supporting financially in order to prove to the farmworkers that they could be independent of outside influences. This was why he rejected a fifty thousand dollar grant from a private group. Manuel and Richard Chávez were so upset that he rejected the grant that they almost quit right then.

They stayed on, however, and traveled around the valley, getting members, while Huerta and Helen did the books and other office work. Initially, they got 212 members to pay dues. But the $3.50

Dolores Huerta, left, registers delegates at the first National Farm Workers Association meeting in September 1962. Huerta was one of the union's founding members.

monthly dues proved too much for the impoverished laborers, and three months later only twelve members were still sending in their dues payment.

So Chávez tried another strategy to get things going, holding fund-raiser barbecues and fiestas that drew thousands of people. This idea publicized their cause widely, and soon they were building up membership again.

Beginning in 1964, the union also began publishing *El Macriado* (which means "The Ill-Bred One" or "The Brat"), an official newspaper that expressed their views and demands, while establishing that the NFWA was not a bracero or communist organization. Much later, in 1983, Chávez also founded the radio station Radio Campesina. When it began, the programs were mostly announcers talking about news events and trying to inspire farmworkers to unionize. In the late 1980s when Chávez's son Paul took over, the emphasis was on South American protest music.

The year 1964 also brought good news for farmworkers: The U.S. Congress passed legislation officially ending federal government support of the Bracero Program.

The War of the Roses and the Grape Strike

Although membership was growing and the financial situation of the NFWA was steadily improving, Chávez felt that the strength of the union was still tenuous in 1965 and he was reluctant to commit to aggressive strikes. He also wanted to be certain he had enough committed union members to support a strike, otherwise it was doomed to fail. Still, he offered his support to a rose harvester named Epifanio Camacho, who wished to protest unfair wages. Chávez offered him advice on how to hold house meetings and recruit strikers. He also published story in *El Macriado*, calling it "The War of the Roses."

When Camacho felt they were ready, the union held a strike against the large rose grower Mount Arbor. Scabs—workers who did not support their fellow laborers—undermined the strike, yet Mount Arbor still decided to grant a wage increase. After the strike was called off, however, Mount Arbor did not give its employees a new contract and Camacho found himself blacklisted, unable to find work.

So when Chávez heard that Filipino immigrants in Delano had organized under AWOC to hold a strike against grape growers in September of 1965, he was nervous. He said:

> I thought the growers were powerful and arrogant, and I judged they were going to underestimate us, but I wasn't afraid of them or their power. I was afraid of the weakness of the people. I knew that the only way we could win was to keep fighting a long time, and I didn't see how we could get that determination.[19]

He knew the NFWA would be called on for support, and he was right. Calling a meeting of the NFWA, he asked the membership what they wished to do. Chávez warned them that there were insufficient strike funds to pay them if they walked off their jobs, and they might have to go without an income for a very long time. Still, the members all cried out, "Huelga!" and so it was decided. The NFWA would strike alongside the AWOC grape workers. What became known as the Great Delano Grape Strike had begun.

Hippies and Flower Children

Chávez's labor movement came at an ideal time in American history when there was considerable support from those later called the Baby Boomers, who were interested in racial, social, and economic justice. Chávez received volunteer support from student organizations such as the Student Nonviolent Coordinating Committee (SNCC) and the Congress of Racial Equality (CORE), as well as from hippies. These were young people, who were part of the free-sex, drug-experimentation, and rock-and-roll culture. Chávez liked their spirit, but usually found them less than helpful to La Causa. He felt they usually spent more time talking and even romanticizing the plight of the poor than being productive. He said:

> We don't let people sit around a room crying about their problems. . . . No philosophizing— *do* something about it. In the beginning, there was a lot of nonsense about the poor farm worker: "Gee, the farm worker is poor and disadvantaged and on strike, he must be a super human being!" And I said, "Cut that nonsense out, all right?"

Quoted in Peter Matthiessen, *Sal Si Puedes: César Chávez and the New American Revolution.* New York: Random House, 1969, p. 115.

Picketing and Boycotts

Strikes against growers could be effective with enough membership support, but Chávez knew of another strategy that could help tip the scales in the NFWA/AWOC strike for better wages from grape growers: a boycott. The plan was to get people, whether or not they belonged to a union, to stop buying grapes, or products made from grapes, from companies that paid unfairly low wages. In 1965 his first target was wine and liquor producer Schenley Industries, but in 1966 the boycott was expanded to include not just the liquor producer, but all the grape growers in California. The strike and boycott strategy attacked growers on two sides: They were losing workers and people were not buying their grapes. They became so desperate that they even hired children to pick grapes while sheriff's deputies stood by and watched. "One of our most powerful nonviolent weapons is the economic boycott," Chávez once asserted. "Alone, the farm workers have no economic power; but with the help of the public they can develop the economic power to counter that of the growers."[20]

César Chávez stands in his office beneath a banner promoting the grape boycott, which urged consumers to stop buying the product from growers who would not pay their workers fair wages.

The strike and boycott drew the attention of a powerful new ally. Walter Reuther, the president of the United Auto Workers union, heard what was going on during an AFL-CIO convention in San Francisco. In a grand gesture of support, Reuther not only walked with picketers but also promised to give them five thousand dollars a month. The NFWA now had a powerful union leader on their side who gained them national attention.

An Independent Union

"I really thought César was crazy. Everybody did but Helen. They had so many children and so little to eat, and that old 1953 Mercury station wagon gobbled up gas and oil. Everything he wanted to do seemed impossible. . . . What impressed me was that even though César was desperate, he didn't want our money, or Teamster money, or AFL-CIO money, or any other money that might compromise him."

Reverend James Drake, on Chávez's decision to form a grassroots union that did not depend on outside financial help. Quoted in Jacques Levy, *César Chávez: Autobiography of La Causa*. New York: Norton, 1975, pp. 162–63.

Other allies followed, including the Student Nonviolent Coordinating Committee (SNCC), an organization some people believed to be a communist front, which resulted in more criticism of the NFWA. Another, even more politically powerful ally came early in 1966, when U.S. senator Robert F. Kennedy publicly announced his support of the farmworkers' unions. As a direct result, more and more people around the country boycotted Schenley wines.

Peaceful Strikes Versus Violent Growers

More support came from unlikely places. While picketing in the fields, union members convinced many scabs to join them. Chávez wisely recruited scabs from different ethnic backgrounds—thus, he found someone of Japanese descent to talk to Japanese scabs, someone who was black to talk to the blacks, a white person to talk to the Okies, and so on. This strategy went a long way in reducing the number of scab workers who would cross the picket line, removing the one last weapon growers had against the local laborers.

Then, to raise union members spirits, an actor named Luis Valdez had an idea. He founded *El Teatro Campesino*, or "The Farm Workers' Theater." Made up primarily of striking immigrant workers, the troupe put on satirical plays that spoofed evil growers. These shows, performed on truck beds where the picketers could watch, were designed to encourage the strikers. The plays did, indeed, boost morale considerably, as well as gain more support from nonunion people.

The growers, for their part, did what they could to break up the strike. They harassed the picketers, sometimes shoving them or even threatening them with shotguns. Sometimes there would be standoffs between the Mexican and Filipino strikers and the growers that turned into fights. Police were called, and on occasion a grower was arrested. However, even in the case or two where a grower was put on trial, he was always acquitted.

Union members were also frequently arrested for no reason, and other unethical tactics were used as well. For example, the local fire chief was asked to inspect the NFWA's headquarters for possible

The March Is a Pilgrimage

For César Chávez, *La Causa* was both a socially and religiously motivated mission. As with the fasts he would later inflict upon himself, he felt the people at large should also demonstrate a willingness to suffer for a righteous cause; there were distinct parallels between his labor marches and religious pilgrimages, which is why he called marches "pilgrimages."

As Chávez stated in a 1966 letter:
Pilgrimage, penance and revolution. The pilgrimage from Delano to Sacramento has strong religio-cultural overtones. But it is also the pilgrimage of a cultural minority who have suffered from a hostile environment, and a minority who means business.

Quoted in Winthrop Yinger, *César Chávez: The Rhetoric of Nonviolence.* Hicksville, NY: Exposition, 1975, p. 107.

fire code violations so that it could be closed down; people who parked their cars at the office had their license plates recorded, and whenever that plate number was seen downtown they were pulled over by police and questioned.

Such treatment, ironically, helped the NFWA's cause. For instance, when police arrested several strikers who were chanting "Huelga!" Chávez announced what had happened while giving a speech at the University of California at Berkeley. Thousands of students in the audience responded by chanting their support for *La Causa*.

March!

Support for the union was snowballing, but still the grape growers were holding firm against the demands for fair pay. Meanwhile, with their partnership working well, the NFWA and AWOC decided to merge in 1966 to form the United Farm Workers Organizing Committee (UFWOC) with backing from the AFL-CIO. Combining the unions resulted in more people and financial

César Chávez, center, testifies during a U.S. Senate Migrant Labor Subcommittee hearing in Sacramento, California, explaining that the Delano grape strike would continue until the growers agreed to bargain with the union, on March 14, 1966.

resources becoming unified in a single purpose.

Although the FBI was investigating the farmers' union, suspecting them of communist ties, other branches of the government were actually helping. The Office of Economic Opportunity had granted the NFWA over a quarter of a million dollars so that the union could fund classes on money management and applying for U.S. citizenship. The grant announcement came as the grape strike was underway, which proved to be bad timing, drawing attention from the Delano town council, which criticized the move. Chávez successfully had the grant money postponed until after the strike so as not to cause further resentment from the local politicians.

As the strike dragged on, morale needed a boost and the cause needed a new burst of energy. The union decided to hold a march, starting on March 17, 1966. More than a march, it was really a pilgrimage, as Chávez called it. The route would take them from Delano all the way to the state capital of Sacramento about 350 miles (649 km) away. The goal was to arrive in Sacramento on Easter Sunday, April 10, and formally deliver a list of grievances to Governor Edmund G. "Pat" Brown. According to Matthiessen:

> The theme was "Penitence, Pilgrimage, and Revolution." Chávez felt from the beginning that the march should be penitential like the Lenten processions of Mexico, an atonement of past sins of violence on the part of the strikers, and a kind of prayer.[21]

The march was also a protest against an insidious strategy being employed by Schenley. Says Matthiessen, the company was "spraying NFWA pickets with poisonous insecticides."[22] Yet another inspiration for the march was the Freedom March led by African American civil rights leader Martin Luther King Jr. in 1963.

Chávez also allowed some of the marchers to carry images of the Virgin of Guadalupe, a move that non-Catholics in the march objected to, including Epifanio Camacho. Camacho was co-captain of the march, but he resigned that position to protest the distinctly Catholic theme.

Despite this disagreement, the march was a big success. Many marchers came and went along the route, just participating in part of the march before they became too weary to continue. When the marchers reached Stockton, they were five thousand strong, although the number dwindled to three thousand by the time they reached Sacramento. Once in town, the marchers paraded through the streets, and the police left them alone, wary of the negative publicity.

Chávez walked the entire distance sick with a fever, with blistered feet and an aching back. The effects of the march on his body were severe and he walked with a cane for days afterward.

Victory

The final blow to the grape growers came a few days before the marchers reached Sacramento. The International Brotherhood of Teamsters union began circulating a false rumor that the Bartenders International Union was going to support the boycott. This would have severely crippled wine and grape sales, so Schenley Industries finally gave up and agreed to negotiate.

So when union leaders and their followers arrived in the state capital, there was much cause for celebration. Chávez, who had temporarily left the march in order to meet with Schenley representatives, returned. As cited in Ferris and Sandoval, "[An] exul-

Dolores Huerta, shown here in 1968 during the grape strike, was a key union leader who supported César Chávez and la causa.

tant throng entered Sacramento, headed by several Chicano flag bearers on horses, wearing black sombreros and dressed in maria-chi garb. The crowd swarmed the capitol steps, where Dolores, wearing a rakish cowboy hat, her face radiant with joy, took the microphone."[23]

Dolores Huerta spoke to the marchers, demanding that the state government "enact a collective bargaining law for the state of California."[24] When Chávez took the podium, however, he made a point to thank everyone and to remind them "that in victory there must be humility."[25]

Continuing the Fight

Schenley Industries was only one of many companies in the region that depended on produce, and Chávez knew that their first significant victory would just be the beginning of a very long struggle. In 1967 the UFWOC next went after Giumarra Vineyards and an even bigger opponent, the DiGiorgio Fruit Corporation, the maker of the popular TreeSweet brand of juices.

For several years, even before they merged, the NFWA and AWOC had been trying to put pressure on DiGiorgio without success because they did not have the resources at the time to strike. After their victory against Schenley, however, the union knew it could take on DiGiorgio. Chávez quickly organized a boycott. He was encouraged when DiGiorgio asked him to come to the negotiating table, but it became apparent this was just a ploy.

While Chávez was in Fresno talking to company representatives, DiGiorgio was busy firing union workers, arresting others, and inviting the Teamsters to recruit employees to its union. Now known to have been a very corrupt union at the time, the Teamsters originated as a labor union for white people and was not likely to press the growers for better wages and living conditions for Hispanic farmworkers. Because the Teamsters was more interested in collecting dues from their members than actually helping them, the growers saw a distinct advantage in replacing Chávez's union with the Teamsters. DiGiorgio's strategy made Chávez nervous. He said:

> [The farm workers] weren't frightened like I was [of the Teamsters], but I knew the complications. I knew,

for example, that five years before, an AFL-CIO strike in the Imperial Valley against Bud Antle, the world's largest lettuce grower, was broken when Antle signed a contract with the Teamsters. DiGiorgio knew it, too.[26]

Redoubling their boycott efforts, the UFWOC spread the word from San Francisco to Los Angeles and all the way to New York City, asking people to boycott DiGiorgio products. Distributing fliers and sending out union representatives in buses all over the country, they gained public support from Americans everywhere. Under this kind of pressure, DiGiorgio permitted the workers to hold an election. They chose the UFWOC over the Teamsters. Defeating a powerful union like the Teamsters made fruit growers and wineries take notice, and soon other companies were negotiating with the UFWOC as well. Chávez's union also got a signed noncompete contract with the Teamsters, who promised they would not challenge it.

King's Assassination

The year 1968 was a bad one for Americans, who lost two important leaders: Robert F. Kennedy and Martin Luther King Jr. After learning of King's assassination on April 4, 1968, Chávez reflected:

I had followed King's actions from the beginning of the bus boycott in Montgomery, when I was organizing the CSO, and he gave me hope and ideas. When the bus boycott was victorious, I thought then of applying boycotts to organizing the Union. Then every time something came out in the newspapers, his civil rights struggle would just jump out of the pages at me.

Although I met some of the people that were working with King and saw him on television, I never talked with him except on the phone. But Martin Luther King definitely influenced me, and much more after his death. The spirit doesn't die, the ideas remain. I read them, and they're alive.

Quoted in Jacques Levy, *César Chávez: Autobiography of La Causa*. New York: Norton, 1975, p. 289.

The Hunger Strike

The long fights against Schenley and DiGiorgio were straining members' resolve. But the fight against Giumarra Vineyards led to an even more frustrating battle. Giumarra was getting around the boycott with the help of other growers. They shipped Giumarra grapes in boxes labeled with the names of other companies, so shoppers could not tell which grapes to avoid buying.

Chávez responded by calling for a boycott against *all* grapes in January 1968. This was, according to Ferris and Sandoval, "a campaign that cut across all age, class, and regional differences, and became the most ambitious and successful boycott in American history."[27]

Fasting and Prayer

"A lot of people thought César was trying to play God, that this guy really was trying to pull a saintly act. Poor César! They just couldn't accept it for what it was. I know it's hard for people who are not Mexican to understand, but this is part of the Mexican culture—the penance, the whole idea of suffering for something, of self-inflicted punishment. . . . In fact, César has often mentioned in speeches that we will not win through violence, we will win through fasting and prayer."

Dolores Huerta, on the misunderstanding many people had about Chávez's motivations for fasting. Quoted in Jacques Levy, *César Chávez: Autobiography of La Causa*. New York: Norton, 1975, pp. 277–78.

The strain was showing in the fields, though, where union workers were being increasingly harassed. More and more, people were pressuring Chávez to use violence to fight back against the police and the grape companies. Chávez refused to consider responding with violence. He feared that physical force would result in the UFWOC losing respect and legitimacy.

Chávez had to make his point somehow, so he followed the example of his hero Gandhi and started a hunger strike on February 13, 1968. He went without food for nearly a month. During this

Senator Robert Kennedy, left, visits a weakened César Chávez at a United Farm Workers rally in March 1968. Chávez was in the midst of the first of several hunger strikes he staged to draw attention to the union's plight.

time, UFWOC members and other supporters, scared they might lose their leader, set up camps to show their support at a place near Delano called Forty Acres, where Chávez and his family had retreated to avoid the media. The tactic worked, and the dissent that had been threatening the unity of the UFWOC dissipated.

At the end of his hunger strike, Chávez was visited by his friend Senator Robert Kennedy to show his support for the union. The UFWOC responded in kind by campaigning in California for Kennedy's presidential bid. On June 4, 1968, the day Kennedy won the California vote, he was assassinated. Chávez could only shake his head sadly and say how senseless the killing was. He had lost a powerful ally who might have become president.

The hunger strike had left Chávez weak, and later in 1968 he was admitted to the hospital for severe back pain, a problem that would plague the union leader off and on for the rest of his life. Slowly regaining his health, Chávez went back to work with a new sense that with national attention came vulnerability. Could he be a target for assassination as Kennedy was? To protect himself and his family, he hired bodyguards. Sometimes he even hired members of the Brown Berets, an organization of urban Hispanics inspired by the African American Black Panthers movement.

Chapter 4

Victories and Defeats

On July 4, 1969, César Chávez was on the cover of *Time* magazine. Having achieved national prominence, Chávez and the UFWOC were positioned to make huge strides in labor justice. Over the next decade or so, there would be significant victories, indeed, but there would also be disappointing setbacks and challenges.

The *Time* article describes Chávez this way:

> La causa's magnetic champion and the country's most prominent Mexican-American leader is César Estrada Chávez, 42, a onetime grape picker who combines a mystical [manner] with peasant earthiness. La causa is Chávez's whole life; for it, he has impoverished himself and endangered his health by fasting. In soft, slow speech, he urges his people—nearly 5,000,000 of them in the U.S.—to rescue themselves from society's cellar. As he sees it, the first step is to win the battle of the grapes. . . .
>
> César Chávez has made the Chicano's cause well enough known to make that goal [of success within

By the late 1960s, César Chávez and his work on behalf of farm laborers had gained national prominence. Time *magazine ran a cover story on Chávez in its July 4, 1969 issue.*

American society] possible. While la huelga is in some respects a limited battle, it is also symbolic of the Mexican-American's quest for a full role in U.S. society. What happens to Chávez's farm workers will be an omen, for good or ill, of the Mexican-American's future. For the short term, Chávez's most tangible aspiration is to win the fight with the grape growers. If he can succeed in that difficult and uncertain battle, he will doubtless try to expand the movement beyond the vineyards into the entire Mexican-American community.[28]

The Grape Fight Continues

On the one hand, 1969 was a bad time for *La Causa* because the victory against DiGiorgio crumbled to dust. The grower sold all its farms to another company, which was then not obligated to honor the contract with the UFWOC. On the other hand, the grape boycott was gaining strength across the United States. Many people were supporting the union and refusing to buy grapes.

The U.S. Department of Defense apparently tried to help the growers by purchasing grapes and sending them to soldiers fighting in Vietnam. They purchased eleven million pounds of grapes that year, but some crew members in the navy threw their supplies overboard in a show of support. The UFWOC extended its strikes to protests at military posts. Another strategy growers would use, though, was to sell their grapes to Europe, where people had no interest or knowledge in what was going on in America's farmlands.

César Chávez, seated left, and grape grower John Guimarra, Jr. prepare to sign a contract to end the grape strike against Guimarra Valley on July 29, 1970. United Farm Workers attorney Jerry Cohen, left, and Bishop Joseph Donnelly review the contract over Chávez's shoulder.

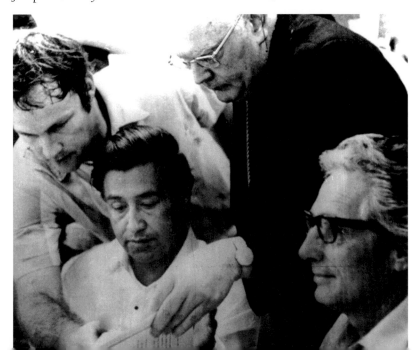

The union extended its request for boycotts to include Canada, as well, and Chávez asked shoppers to not only refuse to buy grapes but also to end their patronage of any store that sold them. Grape growers were now more nervous than ever.

The first grower to give in was Lionel Steinberg, who agreed in April 1970 to raise his workers' salaries. The following July, Giumarra Valley signed a contract, too. The UFWOC was quick to get the word out to their boycotters, telling them they could now purchase grapes from these vineyards. Sales for the companies soared, and when other growers saw this, they contacted Chávez, as well. After five years of striking against grape growers, about 75 percent of the state's farms were unionized.

The Teamsters Muscle In

No sooner had events seemed to take a turn for the better than Chávez was faced with a new problem. The Teamsters union, which had once been the UFWOC's ally against Schenley Industries but had also briefly partnered with the growers, was once again undermining the farmworkers' union. The growers were trying to have the Teamsters recruit UFWOC members to weaken their numbers.

Chávez was trying to return to his preferred methods of slowly organizing members and funds before announcing another strike. The union, drained from the grape strike, needed time to recover. The good news is that the UFWOC victory had drawn tens of thousands of new members to the fold. Chávez began thinking of his next target, which he felt should be the strawberry and vegetable growers in the Salinas Valley. Before they could get organized, however, trouble broke out. The Teamsters turned their backs on their 1967 agreement not to compete with the UFWOC. According to Ferris and Sandoval:

> César . . . returned to Delano to put the final touches on the grape contracts, still hoping there was time to avoid a clash in Salinas. But on the eve of the contract ceremony on July 29, [1970] he found out that the rumors of the Teamster takeover were true. Thirty Salinas growers had already signed the agree-

ments, and more than 175 other vegetable ranchers were waiting in the wings. "They can't get away with this. It's preposterous," Chávez responded furiously. "They're going to have a big fight on their hands. . . . They're not going to sign up our people."[29]

With the help of the U.S. Catholic Bishops' Committee on Farm Labor, which served as mediator, the Teamsters and UFWOC began to talk with each other. Chávez began what he called a fast of penance and thanksgiving during the negotiations. The two unions agreed that the UFWOC could recruit workers in the fields, while the Teamsters could recruit other workers, such as those in the processing plants.

The lettuce growers, however, did not feel bound to this agreement. Author Jan Young writes, "Most admitted that they did not want any union at all among their field workers. If they were going to be forced to accept one, they preferred the Teamsters to the UFWOC, which they considered radical and subversive."[30] Unable to change the growers' minds, Chávez, who was still recovering from his recent six-day hunger strike, declared that the brief moratorium he announced during negotiations were cancelled.

Two Great Honors in 1974

As a faithful Catholic, Chávez was naturally amazed, humbled, and honored when Pope Paul VI granted him a meeting on September 25, 1974. Chávez had decided to travel with his family to Europe that year to try to get consumers there not to buy the grapes American growers were shipping overseas. The Pope agreed to see Chávez and his wife in a private meeting, during which the Pope praised the union leader for his continued insistence on peaceful demonstrations and for championing to improve the lives of the poor. Chávez later described the experience as a "small miracle" for him and a "highlight" in his life.

The year 1974 marked another honor for Chávez, as well, when he received the Martin Luther King, Jr. Nonviolent Peace Prize in Atlanta, Georgia. The prize was presented to him by King's widow, Coretta Scott King.

The Lettuce Strike Turns Violent

The UFWOC's lettuce strike and boycott was the biggest in U.S. history up to that time. It was also the ugliest in terms of violence. The strike was only on its second day, with about five thousand farmhands on the picket lines, when people started punching each other and throwing rocks. Fred Ross, who was still a constant ally of Chávez's, remembered his friend's plea that there be no violence and he ordered the picketers to withdraw.

Chávez Visits Cohen in the Hospital

"When we go in to see Jerry briefly, he seems more concerned for César than for himself. He fears César will be arrested for violating the restraining orders. . . . Then he warns César. If he is put in jail, he should not eat the food. Jerry has learned from one of the California Rural Legal Assistance attorneys that a prison guard poisoned an inmate recently."

Author Jacques Levy in his book, *César Chávez: Autobiography of La Causa*. New York: Norton, 1975, p. 388.

When Jerry Cohen, the union's attorney, visited the farm of lettuce grower Al Hansen to see how the strikers were doing, he was met by a group of burly Teamster men. Hansen reportedly ordered the Teamsters to assault Cohen and those with him. The Teamsters beat Cohen so severely that he had to be taken to the hospital. Chávez recalled:

> Jerry's beating signaled the beginning of Teamster violence against us. And it was pretty much a pattern of what they did in Delano and other places.
>
> There were Teamsters coming and intimidating people, some beatings, some shootings. They beat up four or five lonely pickets where they found them by themselves. They tried to run some people off the road. They threw objects from moving automobiles into the picket lines.[31]

Still insisting on nonviolence, Chávez would tell any picketer who threw a punch or otherwise tried to fight back that they could no longer picket with the union. The fights drew the attention of the courts, however, including one incident when three of Chávez's followers—now often called *Chávistas*—shot a Teamster. In September 1970 a state superior court judge ordered the union to halt the strike. Chávez complied, but as an alternative ordered a lettuce boycott.

Going to Jail

In addition to boycotts and strikes, Chávez became savvy about using the court system, which is why he had hired Cohen as the union's attorney. The UFWOC was now suing growers for unfair practices, including price fixing.

The strategy worked both ways, though, and lettuce grower Bud Antle convinced the court on December 4, 1970, that Chávez was in violation of a court injunction against the strike. So Chávez went to prison. Within days, hoards of his supporters surrounded the jail, along with huge crowds of anti-unionists who repeatedly chanted that the union members were communists. Fighting occasionally broke out, especially when Robert Kennedy's widow, Ethel, visited Chávez on December 6 in a show of support. She had to sneak out a back door after her visit to ensure her safety. Chávez was released on Christmas Eve, and a few months later an appeal found him not guilty.

But Chávez's list of enemies was growing, and it included President Richard Nixon, who supported the Teamsters and growers. In 1971 the pressure became so bad on Chávez that FBI agents uncovered a plot in which several growers had hired trained killers to assassinate him. Fortunately, the conspiracy was thwarted and those involved were arrested.

The UFWOC Becomes the UFW

With increasing threats against him and his family, it was not surprising that in 1971 Chávez moved his union headquarters to a remote, former tuberculosis hospital in the Tehachapi Mountains about an hour's drive south of Delano. He named the headquarters *Nuestra Señora de la Paz* ("Our Lady of Peace"). The move seemed out of character for a man who always said he wanted to work closely with union members, and some criticized him for removing himself from the center of the action.

Increasingly, Chávez was bogged down in administrative work, but it was important work he had to tackle, such as raising funds for medical benefits and pensions, and structuring a formal system to handle membership complaints and establish seniority. By this time, too, the union's membership was expanding beyond the borders of California to include workers in Arizona, Florida, and Texas. In 1972 Chávez renamed the UFWOC the United Farm Workers (UFW), the name by which it is still known today.

Si, Se Puede!

The UFW got its own motto, somewhat unexpectedly. As the fight against the Teamsters raged on, Chávez was fighting a new law passed by Arizona and signed by its governor, Jack Williams. The legislation was a union buster that prevented unions from striking and boycotting, especially during harvest season. After the law passed in 1972, Chávez tried to organize a recall of the governor. His followers told him it was impossible; it could not be done. Chávez replied, "Si, se puede!" (Yes, it can be done!) The assertive statement became the new motto.

Chávez had made that declaration during yet another fast held in protest of the Arizona law. Starving himself was taking a toll, however, and his heart began to suffer. He had to call off his fast after three weeks. Unfortunately, the hunger strike didn't rally enough support to reverse the legislation, although Williams was voted out of office in 1974 and replaced with the state's first Hispanic governor, Raul Castro.

Meanwhile, efforts to support farmworkers in Florida was having mixed results. The UFW campaigned against a law that prohibited the use of hiring halls, which were set up to hire union laborers for farm work, rather than letting growers hire illegal immigrants through contractors. Farm companies responded to the use of hiring halls by campaigning for a "right to work law." The law sounded good on the surface but in reality would have been a blow to the unions. Growers argued that anyone should be allowed to apply for

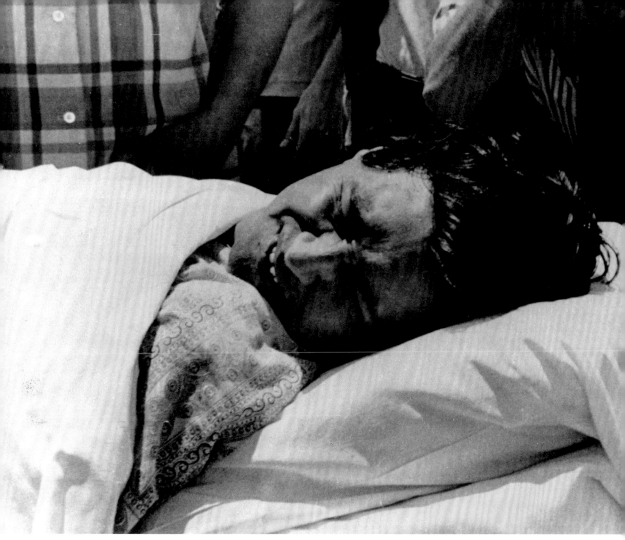

A hunger strike in May 1972 to protest an Arizona law that prevented unions from staging strikes and boycotts at harvest time takes its toll on César Chávez, who required hospitalization to restore his health.

work, whether or not he or she belonged to a union. Chávez and the UFW membership, though, saw this as a way to discriminate against labor union workers. The UFW combined their campaign against the "right to work" law with efforts to increase membership. While they failed to remove the law from the books, they did increase membership.

A side benefit was that their campaigning also brought in the Health Department, which began regular inspections of the labor camps in Florida. The citrus orchards owned there by Coca-Cola were notorious for such bad labor camps conditions that they were the subject of a television documentary.

Losing Proposition 14

Although the union had managed to defeat 1972's Proposition 22, a pro-growers bill, the UFW-supported Proposition 14 was defeated four years later. The failure could be blamed on a combination of the union not getting their message across to the public, and the political savvy of the Dolphin Group, a public relations firm hired by the growers. Part of Proposition 14 would give unions the right to enter farm land to talk to laborers. Television and newspaper ads produced by the Dolphin Group portrayed the bill as a threat to property rights. The ads effectively convinced most voters that Proposition 14 would violate their privacy and so the law was voted down. Authors Susan Ferris and Ricardo Sandoval observed that this defeat was more personally crushing to Chávez than he let on:

> After the defeat of Proposition 14, friends and union workers noticed a change in Chávez. Although in public he remained optimistic about future political victories, his near-religious faith in the ballot box was fading. In private, former union leaders remember, Chávez seemed disillusioned with the initiative process.

Susan Ferris and Ricardo Sandoval, *The Fight in the Fields: César Chávez and the Farmworkers Movement.* New York: Harcourt, Brace, 1997, p. 209.

Ending the Teamsters Fight

The tug-of-war with the Teamsters was not going well for the UFW in 1973 and 1974. The Teamsters' effort to gain contracts was causing UFW membership to steadily decline. Chávez tried to fight back with legal actions, but more often than not the result was simply a drain on the union's coffers. On the other hand, the Teamsters' suffered embarrassment for their heavy-handed approach. In September 1973, for instance, a Teamster executive and managers at two packing companies in Modesto were accused of paying bribes to Teamster thugs who were intimidating UFW members.

That same month, the Teamsters announced they would cooperate with the UFW, letting Chávez's union organize in the fields while the Teamsters would be the union for cannery and processing plant workers. This was an echo of the agreement of 1967, and just as with that agreement, the Teamsters soon were back to attacking the UFW. Author Jacques Levy reported in November 17, 1973:

> AFL-CIO president George Meany accused [Teamsters president Frank] Fitzsimmons yesterday of reneging on their agreement under which the Teamsters would hand over their California farm fields contracts to the UFW. . . . Meany said, "It appears the Teamsters have decided that their interests lie in maintaining the alliance they have created with these employers, rather than in maintaining their integrity as trade unionists."[32]

And so it dragged on for another four long years. The Teamsters, far wealthier than the UFW, was spending one hundred thousand dollars a month by 1974 to recruit farm field-workers. The AFL-CIO, however, was on the UFW's side, and threw their political and financial clout behind Chávez. Finally, in 1977 the Teamsters

César Chávez, left, and Teamsters Union representative M. E. Anderson sign an agreement on March 10, 1977, to end several years of sometimes violent conflicts between farm workers and the Teamsters Union over recruiting practices and areas of influence.

and the UFW admitted they could not go on fighting each other forever. Both sides were suffering from the bitter battle. They signed a new pact on March 10, 1977. The Teamsters finally honored their agreement with the UFW, and the unions joined together to campaign against the growers.

The Political Tide Turns

During the long fight with the Teamsters, Chávez continued the offensive against the grape growers. He staged another march in February 1975 aimed at protesting against the Ernest and Julio Gallo wine company. About fifteen thousand supporters walked from San Francisco, California, to Modesto, California, where the Gallo headquarters was located. The march was held at a good time. Politics in California had taken a significant turn.

Chávez gained an important sympathetic ear in 1974 when Democrat Jerry Brown, who was also a Catholic and a supporter of farmworkers, was elected to the governor's office. Chávez had supported Brown's bid for the governorship, although he often found himself opposing the politically cautious Brown.

Nevertheless, Chávez took the opportunity to work with Brown to get new farmworker-friendly legislation passed. Brown, the UFW, the AFL-CIO, and the Teamsters held an all-night meeting from May 3 through 4 of 1975. Chávez, who was busy supporting the boycott, did not attend and sent attorney Jerry Cohen to represent the UFW. What resulted was a new law called the Agricultural and Labor Relations Act (ALRA), which Governor Brown signed.

In stark contrast to the laws passed in Arizona, the ALRA allowed farm laborers to strike during harvests. Perhaps even more significantly, the law took the power away from growers to select unions for their workers—which had been the cause of so many headaches with the Teamsters—and allow employees to choose the union they wanted to represent them. The governor announced this breakthrough to the media on June 5, 1975:

> I think today marks a victory, not only for the legislature, not only for the farmworkers, but for all the people of California. . . . In my mind [this law] restores great confidence to the ability of the legisla-

United Farm Workers and their supporters picket a liquor store to bring attention to a boycott of wine produced by the Ernest and Julio Gallo wine company in 1975.

tive process and the goodwill of the people to work together even when emotions are running high and solutions seem very far and remote.[33]

Dissatisfaction with the New Bureaucracy

Despite the landmark law, there were still conflicts to be resolved. The ALRA established an oversight board called the Agricultural Labor Relations Board (ALRB) to mediate employer-employee disputes, but the first board included many members who were friends and allies of Chávez. Growers immediately protested that the ALRB was unfairly balanced against them.

The Gallo winery was already resisting the law. It refused to allow UFW representatives onto their grounds to recruit new members and talk with current ones. Growers also did not cooperate with the ALRB. According to author Michelle E. Houle, "The ALRB . . . was forced to operate under exceedingly difficult circumstances, particularly after disgruntled growers provoked a bitter year-long political confrontation with the UFW by blocking the special appropriations the agency needed to support its heavier than expected workload."[34]

Chávez's Life Is Threatened

"I talked to César on the phone from New York. He told me about the threats, and said, 'I've just made up my mind that I know it's going to happen sooner or later. There's nothing I can do.' When I first came back [to California from New York], he was just so damn morbid. In fact, when I got in the office, I sat there crying, because I just felt that he had resigned himself. . . . But as César's health and the security improved, his state of mind did, too."

Dolores Huerta, on seeing a distraught Chávez after he had learned of several threats against him. Quoted in Jacques Levy, *César Chávez: Autobiography of La Causa*. New York: Norton, 1975, p. 292.

Some of the tactics used by the growers were even more reprehensible. As the editors of *The Words of César Chávez* reported:

> Opponents of the ALRB unleashed a textbook example of the use of power to undercut labor laws and to bust unions, engaging in a variety of activities, both legal and illegal, such as burglarizing union offices, placing spies in the UFW, and initiating lawsuits and legislative action.[35]

As the newly established bureaucracy established to help the farmworkers plodded along—in 1976 it even had to close its offices for several months because it had run out of money—Chávez made another attempt to draw attention to the cause against grape growers and spur on action. He started a new march.

Another Long March and Other Steps Forward

Chávez's next march against the grape growers would be the longest march he ever held, but it is much less remembered than the first pilgrimage Chávez led back in 1966. Beginning at the California-Mexico border, the route took him and the other marchers on a thousand-mile journey through much of California.

Chávez, who had been suffering some health problems, including his chronic backache, seemed to thrive on the activity. Write Ferris and Sandoval, "It was on this march, say César's friends and aides, that the middle-aged Chicano warrior appeared to recover some of his monumental vigor, which had been sapped by many months spent on the road, sounding the boycott's message and thumping podiums in disgust over the lack of cooperation from politicians and growers in negotiations over the law."[36]

Unfortunately, the march did not cause grape growers to give in to the union or improve their cooperation with the ALRB, and A UFW-supported law, Proposition 14, which would have given the ALRA more money to operate labor-relation offices, failed. On the other hand, many political candidates who supported the UFW were elected to California offices in 1976.

Chávez and the UFW had also won another victory the year before, when Governor Jerry Brown got a law passed that banned the use of the short-handled hoe, known as *el cortito*, in the fields. The hoe was a notorious tool that forced field-workers to bend over for long hours, inevitably injuring their backs.

By 1977, the UFW's ranks, which had shrunk to only about seven thousand during the height of the fight with the Teamsters, was now back up to around fifty thousand members. However, the boycott on grapes had lasted for so long that the public had lost interest in it and began buying grapes again. Chávez finally decided to cancel the boycott at the end of January 1978.

This marked the beginning of a frustrating period for Chávez when his union seemed to suffer more setbacks than victories.

Chapter 5

The Last Fights for Justice

The loss of public interest in the grape boycott was troubling to Chávez because he feared the same apathy might start to affect UFW members. He knew battling the growers was only half the fight. The farmworkers had to take responsibility for securing a better future for themselves.

Chávez, always looking forward to the future, had spent years thinking about what UFW membership in the future would look like. Since the 1960s, for example, he had been encouraging young men and women to get educations in law, medicine, and other areas so that later, when they became working professionals, they might come back and help the union. This proved to be a wise idea, but Chávez knew, too, that the strength of the union came from having a large following of average laborers.

By the late 1970s, Chávez was sensing that the cause had lost some momentum. He expected some stagnation as the union obtained contracts and UFW members started to feel less urgency about getting better wages and fairer treatment. As Chávez commented:

Once we get contracts and good wages, we know

the tendency will be for the majority to lose interest, unless the Union is threatened or a contract is being renegotiated. The tendency will be for just a few to remain active and involved, while everybody else just holds out until something very big happens. That's true of other unions that we've seen; that's true of other institutions; that's true of our country.[37]

Internal Strife

Just as Chávez had experienced with the CSO years before, the UFW was becoming a more formalized, bureaucratic, and cumbersome organization. Chávez tried to maintain control of the now unwieldy union so that he could still keep an active role in all aspects of the organization. Many people, however, interpreted this as an attempt to have authoritarian control of the UFW. The result was dissent from within, and Chávez began to lose people who had been loyal to him for years. According to authors Jensen and Hammerback in *The Words of César Chávez*:

> Between 1978 and 1981 many prominent leaders left in disagreements with Chávez, among them Gil Padilla, one of the union's founders; Jerry Cohen, the chief legal counsel; Jessica Govea, director of the union's health service board; Marshall Ganz, the union's chief organizer; and Eliseo Medina, a former member of the union's executive board. Much of the union's energy was spent in internal battles rather than in winning union elections and negotiating contracts.[38]

One complaint among union leaders was low pay. Chávez did not seem to grasp the idea that not everyone was like him and happy with low wages for a satisfying job. Chávez even considered bringing in volunteers who would receive no salary whatsoever. Other complaints from union leaders included poorly managed benefits, and some felt that Chávez treated people under him too harshly.

Chávez was also finding himself in trouble for the way he managed union funds. The UFW was becoming increasingly active on the political front and gave large donations to the candidates it supported. A lack of proper bookkeeping led to a twenty-five thousand dollar fine for the union in 1983, when the UFW failed to report some of its donations to the state.

The Growers' Viewpoint

"Chávez doesn't negotiate; he demands. Guided by a master plan based on his ideology, Chávez pays little heed to the basis of labor relations compromise. And while the teamsters are known for their business acumen and shrewd negotiating, the UFW is better known for its rigidity and pressure tactics."

Jack King, a negotiator for the California Farm Bureau Federation, talking about the 1979 lettuce strike. Quoted in Susan Ferris and Ricardo Sandoval, *The Fight in the Fields: César Chávez and the Farmworkers Movement.* New York: Harcourt, Brace, 1997, p. 196.

The Game

One rather bizarre example of Chávez making a mistake with his subordinates was when he initiated a practice called The Game. Modeled after a technique used in drug rehabilitation therapy sessions run by a group called Synanon, The Game required employees to insult each other loudly and directly about what they saw as their colleagues' flaws. Chávez meant it as a way to get grievances out in the open, especially when it came to political opinions. Some members were too leftist for Chávez's taste, and he had been criticized by many Filipino members when he traveled to the Philippines and met with dictator Ferdinand Marcos in 1977. Chávez himself did not feel threatened by other people's political opinions, but he could see that his staff was increasingly argumentative.

The Game made many people very uncomfortable with their work environment and it injured working relationships within the group. On at least one occasion, the object of the attacks was Chávez himself. His son Paul, in fact, took advantage of The Game to finally air a criticism that had long troubled Chávez's family: his absence from their lives while he devoted himself to the union. Chávez no doubt was hurt by such words, but the rules of The Game said he had to take the criticism without protest, which he did.

Some feared that the inventor of The Game, Synanon founder Charles Dederich, was becoming a bad influence on Chávez. Write Ferris and Sandoval, "Chávez's drift toward a more autocratic management style, former staff members say, was . . . inspired by Dederich."[39] Dederich was later proven to be a violent man. In 1978 he and several of his Synanon members were convicted of conspiracy to commit murder for putting a live rattlesnake in the mailbox of a Synanon member who had quit the group. That was the end of Dederich's influence on Chávez.

The Big Lettuce Strike

The growers saw these internal problems at the UFW as a weak point they could use to their advantage. They began to protest to the ALRB that Chávez's union lacked the accountants, lawyers, insurance experts, and other professionals needed to serve its membership properly. The union leader had, indeed, fired half his legal staff to reduce expenses, and he consolidated legal operations in the town of La Paz.

César Chávez addresses striking farm workers in Salinas, California, on March 7, 1979, during a rally in support of the lettuce strike.

The lettuce growers also began resisting Chávez's demands for wage increases. Chávez learned that inflation had eaten away wage gains and he called for another increase: from $3.70 to $5.25 an hour. The amount was staggering for the lettuce companies, and they refused.

The resulting lettuce strike of 1979 proved that Chávez still commanded a powerful union. Sun Harvest was the first company to give in to the UFW's demands after the strike had been in progress for about eight months. The other lettuce growers soon followed, and Chávez had won a major victory that raised workers' wages by over 40 percent.

The win was not without costs, however. Chávez was increasingly concerned about violence breaking out. One violent incident occurred on February 10, 1979. Strike leader Rufino Contreras was shot and killed by a ranch guard. The guard was later cleared of any wrongdoing by the courts. It was not the first time a union member had been killed, but such disturbing events started to have an effect on Chávez's planning as he looked ahead. In particular, he began choosing boycotts over strikes as his preferred method of protest.

Setbacks in the 1980s

Despite its troubles, the UFW seemed to be going strong by 1980. They had settled the dispute with the Teamsters, won major disputes against the lettuce and grape growers, helped pass legislation that allowed workers to choose their own unions, and membership was pushing fifty thousand. Some companies even began offering their field laborers vacation time and medical benefits.

These accomplishments made the UFW arguably the most successful farmworkers' union in U.S. history. If nothing else, it certainly had lasted longer than any other union of its kind. Chávez believed that in order to keep the UFW alive, its mission would have to grow and expand to keep the membership interested and involved. Among the issues he wished to address in the 1980s were the effects of mechanical harvesting on labor, expanded services to members by establishing additional training clinics and cooperatives, and increasing political involvement through lobbying.

Many union members did not like the changes Chávez wanted,

and they either complained that Chávez was managing too many aspects of the union or that he had too many white, college-educated people working for him who did not comprehend what life was like for migrant workers on a farm.

Struggling with the Issue of Illegal Immigrants

"We never worked out a solution with immigrants rights groups. . . . We were saying we wanted immigration laws enforced, and that meant dealing with the INS [Immigration and Naturalization Services], which is like dealing with the devil. César was never happy about that."

Attorney Jerry Cohen, quoted in Susan Ferris and Ricardo Sandoval, *The Fight in the Fields: César Chávez and the Farmworkers Movement.* New York: Harcourt, Brace, 1997, p. 243.

Rebellion began to take root within the union, and it came to a head at the 1981 annual convention when a group from the Salinas branch of the UFW selected officer candidates to run against those selected by union leaders. Chávez responded by accusing the upstart Salinas group of being disloyal to the union, and in protest they walked out of the convention. Chávez soon fired them, which resulted in a lawsuit against the union for illegal termination. The fired employees won the legal action, leaving Chávez and the UFW with a bruised reputation.

Growers and a New Governor Fight the UFW

The early 1980s also saw California growers employing a new strategy to get around the union. Whenever they could, they fired employees who were UFW members, then filled in the openings with illegal immigrants from Mexico who were undocumented workers. All employment was handled indirectly through labor contractors so that the growers could not be blamed.

It was as if the Bracero Program had gone back into effect, although this time, the growers had to be more dishonest about their hiring practices. Then, late in 1986, the U.S. Congress passed the Immigration Reform and Control Act (IRCA). While the new law made hiring undocumented workers illegal, it did grant amnesty to thousands of illegals who had been in America working for an extended time. In addition, it allowed growers to hire foreign labor when they could not find enough local workers. This effectively reversed the 1964 legislation that had forbidden braceros and allowed growers to hire foreigners who were nonunion. The IRCA made many UFW leaders uneasy, but Chávez believed the new, legal population of field hands could boost union membership.

Politically, Chávez and the UFW also suffered setbacks when California Republican governor George Deukmejian took office in 1982. Deukmejian had always been anti-union, and to make matters worse he put another anti-union man, David Sterling, in charge of the ALRB. Governor Deukmejian explained that the move was to

Protesting Poisonous Pesticides

While Chávez used the growers' indiscriminate use of chemicals on crops as a weapon to leverage union deals, it was, more importantly, a genuine concern of his. In the 1980s, Chávez felt increasing guilt that his nonstop work on labor union deals may have isolated him from the daily sufferings of farmworkers, including their poor living conditions and the fact that many of them—especially children—were suffering from the effects of toxic fertilizers and pesticides. He spoke at length on this issue in a 1986 speech, saying in part:

A powerful self-serving alliance between the California governor and the $4 billion agricultural industry has resulted in a systematic and reckless poisoning of not only California farm workers but of grape consumers throughout our nation and Canada. The hard won law enacted in 1975 has been trampled beneath the feet of self-interest. Blatant violations of California labor laws are constantly ignored. And worst of all, the indiscriminate and even illegal use of dangerous pesticides has radically increased in the last decade causing illness, permanent disability, and even death.

César Chávez, speech in 1986. United Farm Workers Papers archive, Wayne State University.

rectify the imbalance at the pro-union ALRB.

The effects of Sterling's leadership were felt quickly in 1982. According to Jensen and Hammerback, "Chávez complained bitterly that the labor board was preventing the union from gaining new members because of delays in investigations and certifications. Early into Deukmejian's first term as governor, the [ALRB] agency nearly imploded."[40] By 1984, the governor cut the ALRB's budget, severely crippling its ability to oversee grower-worker relations.

In retaliation, Chávez called for a new grape boycott, but it was completely ineffective. As stated in *The Words of César Chávez*, "Over the years, the UFW had called more than fifty boycotts, leaving the interested public confused about which if any products were being targeted at any given time. Often, even the union's strongest supporters did not know whether a boycott was in effect or what was being boycotted."[41]

The overuse of the boycott, therefore, had made it an impotent weapon, and growers were successfully shipping as many grapes as ever to consumers.

Chávez Attacks Growers' Use of Pesticides

If Chávez had proved one thing over the years, it was that he was willing to change tactics to get the job done. He was avoiding strikes and picket lines as weapons because of the danger of violence, and boycotting was proving to be less effective. With favoritism for growers in the courts and with representatives in the state capital, legal action was proving difficult, as well. There was still another option, however.

Until 1984 Chávez had aimed *La Causa* at fair wages and a right to organize. This had been a tough enough fight, but there were other issues that had not yet been addressed. In particular, the use by growers of highly toxic pesticides in the fields was a huge concern for field laborers' health. This problem not only affected workers, but also residents who lived near the fields and all Americans who ate the treated produce, and so it was an issue Chávez felt would gain the interest of average consumer.

He brought in Dr. Marion Moses, who had been involved with

César Chávez, third from left, joins UFW members and supporters at a march to protest the use of pesticides on farm crops. Chávez brought national attention to the dangers of pesticides and their negative effects on workers and consumers.

the UFW before as a nurse and had since become a physician, to research the data. Analyzing data in the San Joaquin Valley, she found that people exposed to pesticides and chemical fertilizers were more likely to get cancers such as leukemia, especially young children. Residents of the area were also seeing an increase in birth deformities, such as children being born without limbs. Moses's report was released to newspapers, creating a sensation in the media. The media coverage grew more intense in 1986 with reports of farmworkers suffering from severe chemical burns in a San Joaquin citrus orchard.

With solid data in hand to support his argument, Chávez's boycott on grape growers gained popular support. He also campaigned for legislation that would require farmers to post warning signs on recently sprayed fields, but Governor Deukmejian vetoed it. The growers, meanwhile, fought back with a campaign that said the UFW boycott was political, and if Chávez felt the pesticides were a problem, then he should protest the use of chemicals, not boycott grapes.

The Wrath of Grapes

The chemical burn incident and cancer discoveries inspired Chávez to produce a short documentary in 1987 called *The Wrath of Grapes*, a twist on the title of the 1939 John Steinbeck novel *The Grapes of Wrath* about migrant families, known as "Okies," during the Great Depression (1929–1941). The film focuses on the effects of chemical poisoning on farmworkers, and the UFW sent copies to politicians and the public. However, several women who had appeared in the film protested that the UFW had not told them the money from the video would go to the union and would not help their children, many of whom were suffering from cancer. Soon thereafter a judge banned the UFW from selling or distributing the film.

Meanwhile, economic conditions for migrant farmers were getting worse in the 1980s. Illegal immigrants from Mexico were flooding California as they tried to escape an economic depression caused by a collapse of Mexico's oil industry.

UFW membership was going down, and growers were getting out of their contracts by changing ownership agreements and the names of their orchards and ranches so that UFW contracts no longer applied to them. With rare exceptions, such as a 1983 case in which Rancho Sespe owners were caught changing their company name, most growers got away with the ploy.

Living conditions at migrant camps were declining again, and Chávez took this very personally as a failure on his part. More to punish himself than to bring media attention to the issue, he undertook another lengthy fast.

Losing His Influence?

Chávez fasted from July 16 until August 14, 1988, becoming so weak that doctors feared he was damaging his heart. The union leader isolated himself and did not address the media, so many people did not even know he was fasting again. His self-punishment gained media attention again, however, when several members of the Kennedy family visited him and announced their support of the continuing UFW grape boycott. Then, on August 14, civil rights leader and, at that time, a candidate for the presidency, Jesse Jackson came to Chávez's bedside and convinced him to end the fast. As a symbolic gesture, Jackson took over Chávez's fast for three days, then passed it on to others. Afterward, on August 21, Chávez made a speech at Pacific Lutheran University explaining his motivations:

> Do we really carry in our hearts the plight of the farm workers and their children? Do we feel deeply enough the pain of those who labor every day in the fields with these pesticides? Do we know the heartache of families whose loved ones have been lost to cancer, who fear for the lives of their children, who are raising children with deformities, who agonize over the outcome of their pregnancies, who ask in fear, "Where will the deadly plague strike next?"
>
> Do we feel their pain deeply enough? I know I didn't. And I was ashamed.[42]

Rev. Jesse Jackson, right, convinced César Chávez to end yet another hunger strike when he visited the union leader on August 14, 1988, agreeing to stage a fast himself for three days as a gesture of support.

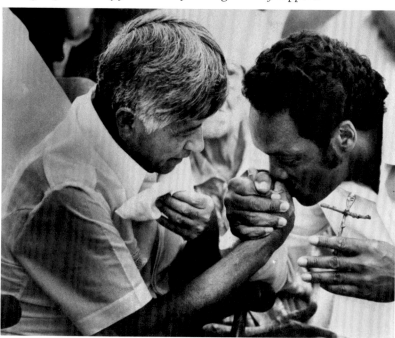

Eulogy for Juana Chávez

Chávez's mother was a lifelong inspiration and model for him, and in his eulogy at her funeral he talked about all the ways in which she had led an exemplary Christian life. In some ways, at least some of the words he offered about his mother could have been applied to him at his own funeral. Chávez said:

We are here today to say that true wealth is not measured in money or status or power. It is measured in the legacy we leave behind for those we love and those we inspire. We are here today because our lives were touched and moved by her spirit of love and service. That spirit is more powerful than any force on earth. It cannot be stopped. Death comes to us all and we do not get to choose the time or the circumstances of our dying. The hardest thing of all is to die rightly. Juana Chávez died rightly. She served her God and her neighbor.

César Chávez, eulogy at his mother's funeral on December 18, 1991. United Farm Workers Papers archive, Wayne State University.

Neither the fast nor the boycott was having any measurable effect on fruit and vegetable sales by 1989. Chávez retreated to La Paz to recover, but an accidental fall in 1989 fractured his wrist and bruised him seriously. When he finally recovered fully, he returned to the campaign trail.

Last Successes and Honors

For the next four years, Chávez seemed to be back to his old self, tirelessly fighting to advance *La Causa*. He made a significant breakthrough in the spring of 1990 when Mexican president Carlos Salinas de Gortari agreed to provide medical benefits to Mexican nationals working in America. Later that year, the president honored Chávez by presenting him with prestigious Order of the Aztec Eagle. The award seemed all the more fitting because the eagle was the UFW's symbol.

Finally, in 1990, the extended grape boycott seemed to be having some impact, too, with growers reporting a decline in sales that year.

Chávez's involvement with the pesticide and fertilizer issue led to his gaining additional support from the growing environmental movement, as well as from consumer advocates such as Ralph Nader. They campaigned in 1990 for California's Proposition 128, which was intended to reduce the use of chemicals in farms and industries. The proposal did not pass, but Chávez remained undaunted. In fact, friends and family noted that he seemed to get a second wind and was working more enthusiastically than ever.

In 1992 Chávez focused his boycott campaigns on the issue of living conditions in labor camps. This time, he had mixed results. While he helped farmworkers get a pay increase, he won no new union contracts.

The early 1990s brought heavy personal blows for Chávez as well. His mother died on December 14, 1991, and his longtime friend, mentor, and union supporter Fred Ross died of cancer on September 27, 1992.

The funeral for Fred Ross had one positive side effect: All the people from the early days of Chávez's union, and from his CSO days, came to say their good-byes. Afterward, Chávez was hopeful that the arguments between him and once-stalwart friends like Gil Padilla and Jerry Cohen could be put aside.

Chávez, however, did not have enough time to see that dream come true.

Gone Too Soon

In early 1993, Chávez was in Arizona on UFW business and decided to visit his family's old home in Yuma, where he had spent a happy childhood before the bank took it away and he and his family became migrant workers. The former little family farm and business was now owned, ironically, by one of the country's biggest lettuce growers, Bruce Church Incorporated.

Bruce Church had filed a lawsuit against the UFW that had been dragging on since the 1980s. In April 1993 Chávez returned to California for the Church trial and to visit a friend and UFW board member named David Martinez who lived in San Luis, California. On April 22, Chávez spent the day in court giving testimony then returned to Martinez's house where he ate dinner and later went to bed to read. The next morning, Martinez discovered that Chávez

Mourners follow the simple pine casket of César Chávez at his funeral in Delano, California on April 29, 1993. An estimated 40,000 people attended the event.

had died peacefully in his sleep.

Martinez called the paramedics and then Chávez's family to tell them the bad news. Chávez's brother Richard built a plain pine coffin for Chávez, just as Chávez had long ago requested.

The funeral was held in Delano on April 29, 1993. An estimated forty thousand people attended. Many who had had disagreements in the past with Chávez came to honor him, and everyone reflected on all that he had accomplished in his sixty-six years.

César Chávez's greatest fear was that the United Farm Workers would crumble after his death, but the union survives to this day, and keeps *La Causa* alive.

Epilogue

The strength and membership of the United Farm Workers have waxed and waned over the decades. Membership was at its height in the 1970s, when it roared to a healthy fifty thousand people. At the time of César Chávez's death in 1993, it was about twenty thousand. Arturo Rodriguez, husband of Chávez's daughter Linda, took up the eagle banner from the fallen leader. Rodriguez, though just as devoted to *La Causa* as the union's founder, was a very different type of leader. College educated, he had a graduate degree in social work from the University of Michigan. This education seemed to make him more appealing to the Anglo business leaders who ran most of the country's corporate farming operations.

One of the first tasks Rodriguez pursued was to rebuild UFW membership. He did this through a couple of strategies, including partnerships with other union organizations and a new tactic he called "master contracts." In 1993, the year Chávez died, Rodriguez had already accomplished a coup by establishing a partnership with a group of Mexican Indian organizations. Mixtecs, as they are called by some, make up a small but significant minority of about 10 percent of farm laborers in California, and so they represented a boost to UFW ranks.

After a 1995 strike against VCNM Farms that resulted in the grower employing the old strategy of declaring bankruptcy, firing UFW workers, and then reopening its strawberry business under a new name, Rodriguez came up with his master contract idea. He negotiated a deal with all the shipping companies that hauled strawberries and got them to agree not to work with growers who did not have UFW contracts. The campaign, completed in 1996, was a huge success.

Rodriguez, of course, was not forging ahead alone. The union still enjoyed the benefits of Dolores Huerta's considerable skills

Arturo Rodriguez, right, took over leadership of the United Farm Workers after César Chávez's death in 1993. Rodriguez is Chávez's son-in-law.

and experience, as well as those of Richard Chávez and other UFW loyalists.

Together, they continued to follow the course Chávez had established of nonviolence and determined pressure against the growers. A significant victory came in 1994 when the union once again defeated wealthy grape grower Ernest and Julio Gallo, which had continued to frustrate the UFW's efforts to hold union elections for Gallo workers. Gallo hired an expensive staff of lawyers and tried to intimidate their employees, but the farmworkers held a strike anyway and won better treatment from the winery.

Three years later, the dispute with Bruce Church ended when an Arizona judge ruled that the UFW did not have to pay an early judgment of 5.4 million dollars against them. The grower finally relented in 1997 and signed a contract with the union.

The Immigration Issue

Such victories showed that the UFW could continue to move forward under Rodriguez's leadership. One of the biggest challenges in recent years has been the immigration issue. A *Washington Post* editorial in 2007 estimated that between eight hundred thousand and a million farmworkers in the United States, most from Mexico, were illegal aliens.[43] Illegal aliens are a problem for the UFW, because they are paid under the table (that is, paid in cash that is not reported to the government) for less money than is required under union contracts.

In 2007 a bill known as AgJOBS received considerable debate in the U.S. Congress. It is aimed at granting amnesty to about eight hundred thousand illegal immigrant farm laborers who have shown they are productive, law-abiding workers. Growers all over the United States increasingly employ illegal workers because they are cheaper to employ than legal workers (U.S. citizens) who are protected by federal wage laws and union contracts.

In a compromise, the bill was changed to allow growers to roll back minimum salaries to 2003 levels. Rodriguez commented on the agreement: "They didn't get everything they wanted, we didn't get everything we wanted. . . . But we're happy with what we got, and we're going to push to keep that compromise intact. You have to be realistic what you ask of farm workers. . . . In the end they are going to realize what we've come up with makes a lot of sense."[44]

Helen Chávez, center, accepts the Presidential Medal of Freedom from President Bill Clinton in honor of her husband on August 8, 1994

The AgJOBS bill became part of the immigration law package in 2007. It was just one more accomplishment among many made in the twenty-first century by the UFW. The union's Web site proudly notes some of their more recent victories:

> New laws and regulations aiding farm workers the UFW won since 1999 range from seat belts in farm labor vehicles and fresh protections for workers cheated by farm labor contractors to an historic binding mediation law and new pesticide protections. The UFW also convinced Republican Gov. Arnold Schwarzenegger in 2005 to issue an emergency regulation preventing further heat deaths of farm workers and all outdoor employees, which was made permanent in 2006 thanks to UFW pressure. In 2006 the UFW won legislation guaranteeing unemployment benefits for seasonal workers in Washington state.[45]

Chávez Remembered

While the mission continues for the UFW, César Chávez remains an enduring symbolic figure. His example of nonviolent struggles for the fair treatment of farmworkers continues to be honored years after his death.

Schools and roads have been named after Chávez, and in 2002 a new hybrid rose was named after the union leader as well. In 1994, the year after Chávez died, President Bill Clinton presented Helen Chávez with America's highest civilian honor, the Medal of Freedom, to honor her late husband. In 2000 California governor Gray Davis declared Chávez's birthday, March 31, to be an official state holiday called César Chávez Day. Since then, initiatives were also proposed by UFW members to create state holidays in Texas, Arizona, New Mexico, Michigan, Colorado, Illinois, and Wisconsin. His union has also been campaigning for a national César E. Chávez Day.

While all these honors are well deserved, a far greater reward for Chávez's lifelong devotion to *La Causa* would be the much more difficult achievement of the elimination of rural poverty in America. As he once said:

In 2003 the U.S. Postal Service issued a postage stamp in honor of César Chávez.

Political power alone is not enough. . . . All the time and the money and effort haven't brought about any significant change whatsoever. Effective political power is never going to come, particularly to minority groups, unless they have economic power. And however poor they are, even the poor people can organize economic power.[46]

Notes

Introduction: The Farmworkers' Champion

1. César Chávez, speech to the Commonwealth Club of San Francisco, California, November 9, 1984. United Farm Workers Papers archive, Wayne State University.

Chapter One: A Migrant Childhood

2. Quoted in Richard W. Etulain, ed., *César Chávez: A Brief Biography with Documents*. New York: Palgrave, 2002, pp. 46–50.
3. Quoted in Etulain, *César Chávez*, pp. 46–50.
4. Quoted in Jonathan A. Brown, *César Chávez*. Milwaukee, WI: World Almanac Library, 2004, p. 13.
5. Richard J. Jensen and John C. Hammerback, introduction to *The Words of César Chávez*, eds. Richard J. Jensen and John C. Hammerback. College Station, TX: Texas A&M University Press, 2002, pp. xviii–xix.
6. César Chávez, speech to the Building Industry Association of Northern California, November 21, 1991. United Farm Workers Papers archive, Wayne State University.
7. Quoted in Etulain, *César Chávez*, pp. 46–50.
8. Brown, *César Chávez*, p. 8.
9. Quoted in Etulain, *César Chávez*, p. 36.

Chapter Two: Becoming a Leader

10. Quoted in Jacques Levy, *César Chávez: Autobiography of La Causa*. New York: Norton, 1975, p. 89.
11. Quoted in Levy, *César Chávez,* p. 87.
12. Quoted in Susan Ferris and Ricardo Sandoval, *The Fight in the Fields: César Chávez and the Farmworkers Movement*. New York: Harcourt, Brace, 1997, p. 50.
13. Quoted in Levy, *César Chávez*, p. 106.
14. Quoted in Levy, *César Chávez*, p. 129.
15. Quoted in Levy, *César Chávez*, p. 147.

16. Quoted in Etulain, *César Chávez*, p. 30.

Chapter Three: La Causa

17. Quoted in Levy, *César Chávez*, p. 160.
18. Peter Matthiessen, *Sal Si Puedes: César Chávez and the New American Revolution*. New York: Random House, 1969, pp. 40–41.
19. Quoted in Levy, *César Chávez*, p. 183.
20. Quoted in Levy, *César Chávez*, p. 201.
21. Matthiessen, *Sal Si Puedes*, p. 127.
22. Matthiessen, *Sal Si Puedes*, p. 127.
23. Ferris and Sandoval, *The Fight in the Fields*, p. 122.
24. Quoted in Ferris and Sandoval, *The Fight in the Fields*, p. 122.
25. Quoted in Ferris and Sandoval, *The Fight in the Fields*, p. 123.
26. Quoted in Levy, *César Chávez*, p. 224.
27. Ferris and Sandoval, *The Fight in the Fields*, p. 139.

Chapter Four: Victories and Defeats

28. *Time*, "The Little Strike That Grew to La Causa," *Time*, July 4, 1969. www.time.com/time/magazine/article/0,9171,840167,00.html.
29. Ferris and Sandoval, *The Fight in the Fields*, p. 162.
30. Jan Young, *The Migrant Workers and César Chávez*. New York: Julian Messner, 1972, p. 175.
31. Quoted in Levy, *César Chávez,* p. 385.
32. Levy, *César Chávez*, pp. 515–16.
33. Quoted in Ferris and Sandoval, *The Fight in the Fields*, p. 200.
34. Michelle E. Houle, ed., *César Chávez*. Farmington Hills, MI: Greenhaven Press, pp. 75–76.
35. Jensen and Hammerback, *The Words of César Chávez*, p. 88.
36. Ferris and Sandoval, *The Fight in the Fields*, p. 201.

Chapter Five: The Last Fights for Justice

37. Quoted in Levy, *César Chávez*, p. 536.
38. Jensen and Hammerback, *The Words of César Chávez*. p. 89.

39. Ferris and Sandoval, *The Fight in the Fields*, p. 213.

40. Ferris and Sandoval, *The Fight in the Fields*, p. 230.

41. Jensen and Hammerback, *The Words of César Chávez*, p. 111.

42. Quoted in Jensen and Hammerback, *The Words of César Chávez*, p.168.

Epilogue

43. *Washington Post*, "Rot in the Fields: As Farmworkers Become Scarcer, Congress Dithers," *Washington Post*, December 3, 2007. www.washingtonpost.com/wp-dyn/content/article/2007/12/02/AR2007120201593.html.

44. Quoted in David Rogers, "Immigration Overhaul May Hit Farms," *Washington Post*, May 10, 2007. http://online.wsj.com/article_email/SB117876355952498047-lMyQjAxMDE3NzE4MDcxNjAzWj.html.

45. United Farm Workers, "Recent Successes," United Farm Workers. www.ufw.org/_board.php?b_code=about_suc#125.

46. Quoted in Levy, *César Chávez*, p. 537.

Important Dates

1927
César Chávez is born Césario Estrada Chávez on March 31 near Yuma, Arizona.

1937
Chávez's family loses their farm and home on August 29. The family begins a life as migrant farmworkers.

1944
Chávez joins the U.S. Navy and serves for two years.

1948
Chávez marries Helen Fabela on October 22.

1952
Chávez begins his active association with the CSO and Fred Ross becomes his mentor.

1962
Chávez resigns from the CSO, and founds the NFWA.

1965
The NFWA votes to go on its first big strike. A boycott against grape grower Schenley Industries begins.

1966
The NFWA and AWOC merge to form the UFWOC. Chávez organizes his first big march, which he calls a pilgrimage.

1970
Chávez launches a strike against lettuce growers.

1972
The UFWOC becomes the UFW, the name by which the union is still known today.

1973

After several contracts with the UFW expire, the Teamsters move in to get labor deals with the growers. This begins a long battle between the two unions.

1975

California governor Jerry Brown signs the Agricultural Labor Relations Act, which creates the Agricultural Labor Relations Board.

1977

On March 10 the Teamsters and the UFW call a truce and agree not to compete for labor union memberships.

1979

The big lettuce strike begins, which is complemented by a call for a nationwide boycott on California lettuce.

1984

California governor George Deukmejian cuts the ALRB's budget; Chávez responds by calling for another grape boycott.

1987

Chávez produces the *Wrath of Grapes*.

1988

From July 16 to August 14, Chávez holds his last and most grueling fast.

1992

Chávez leads his longest protest march yet, but it receives considerably less publicity than earlier marches.

1993

Chávez dies on April 23 at a friend's home.

1994

Chávez receives the Medal of Freedom posthumously.

2000

March 31 is declared César Chávez Day in California.

For More Information

Books

Beth S. Atkin, *Voices from the Fields: Children of Migrant Farmworkers Tell Their Stories*. New York: Little, Brown, 1993. Atkin interviews farmworkers of all ages, letting them tell their stories of hardship, hope, and sometimes success in finding a better life.

Susan Samuels Drake, *Fields of Courage: Remembering César Chávez and the People Whose Labor Feeds Us*. Santa Cruz, CA: Many Names Press, 1999. A combination of memoir and poetry, this book is written by a woman who was a member of the UFW and knew Chávez personally.

Michelle E. Houle, ed., *César Chávez*. Farmington Hills, MI: Thomson/Gale, 2003. An anthology of essays collected from books and articles discussing the history and legacy of César Chávez and his work.

David Seidman, *César Chávez: Labor Leader*. New York: Franklin Watts, 2004. A biography on Chávez written for younger readers.

Web Sites

César E. Chávez Foundation (www.Chávezfoundation.org). This Web site supports the mission of the foundation in keeping Chávez's memory alive and inspiring people to become educated and improve themselves and their communities.

United Farm Workers (www.ufw.org). This is the official Web site of the union Chávez founded. Here readers can learn all about the current activities of the UFW, including news releases and campaign information.

Index

Picture Credits

About the Author

Kevin Hile is a freelance writer, editor, and Web site designer based in Michigan. A graduate of Adrian College, where he met his wife, Janet, he has been a reference book editor for almost twenty years. While an editor for Gale, he worked on series such as *Black Writers*, *Hispanic Writers*, and *Contemporary Authors New Revision*. As a freelancer, he has written *Animal Rights* (Chelsea House, 2004), *Dams and Levees* (KidHaven Press, 2007), *Centaurs* (KidHaven Press, 2008), and *Little Zoo by the Red Cedar* (MSU Press, 2008). He was recently named vice president of Web design and publications for Media Matters of Michigan.